HOW WORK WORKS

ALSO BY MICHELLE P. KING

*The Fix: Overcome the Invisible Barriers That Are
Holding Women Back at Work*

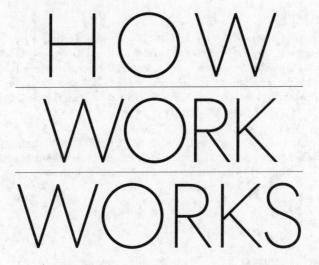

HOW
WORK
WORKS

**The Subtle Science of Getting Ahead
Without Losing Yourself**

DR. MICHELLE
PENELOPE KING

HARPER
BUSINESS

An Imprint of HarperCollins*Publishers*

HarperCollins books may be purchased for educational, business, or sales promotional use. For information, please email the Special Markets Department at SPsales@harpercollins.com.

FIRST EDITION

Designed by Bonni Leon-Berman

Library of Congress Cataloging-in-Publication Data

Names: King, Michelle P., 1982- author.
Title: How work works : the subtle science of getting ahead without losing ourself / Michelle P. King.
Description: First edition. | New York, NY : HarperCollins, [2023] |
  Includes bibliographical references.
Identifiers: LCCN 2023002244 (print) | LCCN 2023002245 (ebook) | ISBN 9780063224575 (hardcover) | ISBN 9780063224582 (ebook)
Subjects: LCSH: Career development. | Employee rules. | Work environment.
Classification: LCC HF5381 .K5866 2023 (print) | LCC HF5381 (ebook) | DDC 650.1--dc23/eng/20230621
LC record available at https://lccn.loc.gov/2023002244
LC ebook record available at https://lccn.loc.gov/2023002245
                    23 24 25 26 27 LBC 5 4 3 2 1

This book is my gift to anyone who wants to be seen, heard, and valued for who they are. Pass it on.

CONTENTS

PREFACE

Tree canopies block the sunlight. In the Fishlake National Forest in Utah, forty-eight thousand towering quaking aspen trees—known for their bright yellow color in the fall and the quaking sound as the wind passes through their leaves—stand together as they have done for centuries upon centuries. The oldest quaking aspen is fourteen thousand years old. How do trees like these aspens survive cold winters, long summers, drought, and insect attacks for so many years?

Researchers initially believed such trees survived for so long because they could outcompete other trees for sunlight, water, and nutrients. But this isn't true. New research has found that trees have learned how to cooperate and depend on one another for survival. Trees communicate through an underground fungal network by sending chemical, hormonal, and slow-pulsing electrical signals to let other trees know if they need water, are in distress, or are under attack by a colony of ants. Other trees then alter their behavior by doing things like pumping sugar into the network to support a tree in distress. A forest isn't simply a collection of trees—it's a community. Every tree belongs to the community by having a place to stand within it.

Trees also communicate through the air. They use pheromones or other scent signals to connect, ask for help, and share what they need because this is how they survive—together. Trees stay alive because they recognize that they belong to one another. Trees harness the power of the collective to ensure their survival by literally reading the air.

An ecosystem of trees is very much like a workplace. For the past twenty years, I have studied how workplaces work, which is something I believe we should all care deeply about. Over an average lifetime, a person will spend around ninety thousand hours at work, which equates to thirteen years. To put this in perspective, humans spend just over one year socializing over the average lifetime. Therefore, where and how we work has a huge role to play in our happiness and overall life satisfaction.

For this reason, I have dedicated my career to studying organizational culture and working with leaders to make workplaces work better for everyone. I have worked with startups, medium-sized corporations, nonprofits, international organizations, and large multinational companies worldwide. I have worked for organizations where I was proud to be a part of the company culture. And I have also worked at companies whose cultures were so toxic that many departments were wiped out due to some catastrophic combination of terminations and resignations.

I am an expert on workplace cultures. I have spent nearly the same amount of time in workplaces as I have in academia. I earned two undergraduate degrees, a master's in organizational psychology, an MBA, and a PhD in management and organizational development.

Based on my work, I know for sure that at one time or another, most of us have lost our belief in work. We have felt the pain of being excluded from informal networks, the stress of trying to keep up with the pace of change, or burnout after putting in countless hours to get the next promotion, only to be overlooked or disillusioned with cutthroat corporate cultures. We are tired of accepting the myth that individual advancement must come at a cost to ourselves and the people we work with.

"I want my workplace to change, but there isn't anything I can do to change it," a manager once said to me with complete sincerity. But we *are* our workplaces. Saying there is nothing we can or should do to change is like assuming aspens have stayed alive for so long by outcompeting one another. Just like a tree is part of a forest, our workplaces are communities—an intricate network of people who rely on one another to survive and flourish. So understanding how to make your workplace work for you starts with understanding your place within it. This book details what it takes to advance at work but, more important, how we derive fulfillment from what we do and contribute beyond a job description. I hope that every reader will understand why our collective survival—much like a tree depends on its forest—is determined by our ability to read the air.

INTRODUCTION

A businessman in Kyoto was in a lunch meeting with his new client. After cordial exchanges, they got down to business. After a while, the client complimented the businessman's watch. Proud and pleased, the man looked at his watch, smiling, marveling at the features of the fancy piece while retelling the story of buying it. The client's face fell, unimpressed by the tale, and he became disengaged in further business discussion. Wondering what he had said wrong, the man studied his watch again, and he noted the time and realized their meeting had gone over the scheduled hour. He had missed the client's subtle cue to wrap up the conversation.

The businessman shared his experience on Twitter, and the tweet went viral because his experience is something we can all relate to. So many of us struggle to know how to manage the informal interactions and experiences of work. For example, do you know (without looking at your watch) when a meeting is nearly over? Do you know when it is the right time to ask for a raise? Do you understand the subtext of what is being said or not said? Can you read the subtle meaning behind someone looking at their watch? The informal side of working life is challenging to manage because it is invisible.

Think about the first job you ever had. How did you learn to do your job? All the official work rules—like the hours you need to work and most of the tasks you need to complete—are explicitly clear because they are written down or communicated in a policy, employee handbook, or job description. But there is another side to working life that doesn't get communicated—the informal rules, which include the norms, expectations, and behaviors that govern how things get done. For example, when you start out in your workplace, you might observe how people interact and what behavior gets rewarded. Your coworkers might welcome you over Zoom, take you out for coffee, or schedule a virtual lunch to get to know you. Each of these observations and interactions helps you piece together *how* your workplace works.

The Japanese have a term for understanding the how of work or reading the shared norms of social situations, *"Kuuki wo yomu,"* which translates to "read the air." The Japanese businessman failed to read the air and wrap up the meeting, which is so unusual in Japan that he felt the need to tweet about his mistake. In Japanese culture, learning to read the air is about grasping the subtext of what is being communicated beyond words, interpreting nonverbal cues, and being mindful of the broader context.

But reading the air is something a lot of cultures are familiar with. I have lived in numerous countries and heard various phrases to describe the ability to understand the informal side of working life. For example, in America, I would listen to my colleagues talk about the need to "read the room," whereas in England, my coworkers refer to "taking the room's temperature." Other standard references include "read between the lines" and learning the "unwritten rules" of working life. These phrases may be used differently in different contexts, but ultimately, they refer to the same thing: *your ability to understand and interpret other people's feelings, needs, and intentions so that you can manage your informal interactions with them.*

Reading the air is not just about knowing the shared norms that govern our everyday interactions. It also includes a deep understanding of your work environment regardless of the setting. Many business leaders I have worked with refer to reading the air as judgment, organizational awareness, or political skill. They argue this ability is the secret sauce to career advancement and success—from the ability to work with anyone to understanding the inner workings of an organization's culture to getting paid what you are worth—if you know how to read the air, you know how to get the job done.

Being able to read the air is about understanding the *how* of work.

Throughout this book, you will venture on a journey of self-discovery as you find out how to read the air and connect with your workplace, your colleagues, and even yourself. This book will demystify "the air" and reveal the unwritten rules for managing the how of work. In discovering how to manage the informal side of working life, you will gain the ability to work anywhere because you'll know how most workplaces work.

The Other Side

In an old Zen story, a youthful monk travels home when he comes across a long, snaking river that seems to go on forever. The young monk cannot see a way of crossing the river. He stands on the bank and tries to find a way to get across. At a loss, he decides to give up. As he turns to leave, he spots an old Zen master standing on the opposite side of the riverbank. He calls out to the Zen master, "Oh, master, I am stranded here. Can you tell me how I may get across to the other side?"

The Zen master smiles at him curiously. Then he turns and looks up and down the river before shouting back, "My good fellow, you are on the other side!"

Over the last two decades, hundreds of articles, studies, and books have examined the challenges we will likely encounter in the future world of work. Collectively these commentaries paint a scary picture of the future. Robots will take our jobs! AI will replace humans! Automation will destroy most jobs! Globalization and technological advancements will change the world of work as we know it forever!

The only problem with these arguments is that the future is already here.

We are already on the other side of the Fourth Industrial Revolution. Automation, AI, and universal interconnectivity are transforming how we work. Complex, critical tasks that require a high level of precision are becoming extensively automated. For example, in a Fanuc plant in Oshino, Japan, industrial robots produce industrial robots supervised by a staff of only four workers per shift. AI is replacing human thought. Olly, an AI assistant created by the technology company Emotech, is like Amazon's Alexa. Still, with one significant difference—Olly has a personality that evolves to become more like its owner, thanks to machine learning algorithms. Technological advancements changing how we work are nothing new. But what most researchers agree *is new* is the accelerated pace of change.

Before the pandemic, it was widely agreed that technological advancements would transform the world of work at a pace we have never experienced before. Likewise, the twenty-first century will be known for the speed and range of technological advancements transforming how we do our jobs. These changes are already upon us. The problem is that we don't know what skills or capabilities we will need to navigate these changes.

And we know it. The Hopes and Fears 2021 report by the consulting firm PricewaterhouseCoopers, which includes a survey of 32,500 employees, found that 60 percent of participants were worried that automation will put their jobs at risk, and 40 percent of respondents believed their job will be obsolete within the next five years. To respond to these challenges, we need to develop new skills, which is why the report found that 77 percent of respondents were ready to learn new skills or completely retrain. But what skills do we need to learn? If we are, in fact, on the other side, what do we need to know to navigate our new world of work?

Like most people, I, too, am worried about the future of my work. Until I researched the topic, I assumed that two decades of experience in my field and five degrees would be enough to sustain my career progression. However, in 2020, when the pandemic hit, very few of us anticipated the pace and extent to which jobs would change. Covid forced businesses to manage the uncertainty by redesigning work processes or increasing the speed of automation, which transformed a lot of jobs and put many others at risk. In 2021, approximately 25 percent more workers than previously estimated had to switch jobs due to remote work, e-commerce, and automation, according to a McKinsey survey of eight hundred senior executives. This study also found that 60 percent of executives invested in automation and AI either somewhat or significantly. Reasons included deploying automation and AI in warehouses, grocery stores, call centers, and manufacturing plants to reduce workplace density and cope with surges in online shopping due to the pandemic. The McKinsey report estimated that one in sixteen workers will need to find a different occupation by 2030, up by 12 percent from prepandemic estimates. Importantly, however, only 6 percent of companies expected their workforce in the United States and Europe to shrink because of automation and AI.

Most of us fear that machines will take our jobs, but what is much more likely, at least in the coming decades, is that machines will change *how* most of us work. This means we must cultivate the skills needed to meet these changes head-on.

In 2015, when I headed up innovation and technology for the United Nations Entity for Gender Equality (UN Women), I worked with thirty private-sector companies like Facebook, General Electric, and SAP to look at how we could use technology and innovation to advance equality and equity. As part of this effort, I researched how the future world of work will require new ways of working. I found that most companies accept the nature of jobs and that workplaces will change, but most don't know what this means for their employees. We are on the other side, but we need to understand what that means for *how* we work.

Transformation 1: Increased Technical Roles

There are four transformations most workplaces are experiencing. First, specialist technical roles like data scientists, programmers, UI designers, and security analysts will continue to grow. These roles are growing at twice the rate of the overall job market. These roles are highly valuable and complex. They require a wide range of skills from different disciplines like website and software design, user experience, data analysis, and marketing, so they also pay 20–40 percent more than nontechnical roles.

Take marketing and public relations, for example, where there is an increasing demand for digital marketing manager roles requiring technical skills like data analytics and creative skills like branding and advertising. These roles cover a broad range of disciplines, and as such, they often call for exceptional teamwork and collaboration.

For example, a digital marketing manager might work with the information technology department, branding, sales, supply chain, and e-commerce team. The interesting thing about these roles is that despite requiring high levels of technical capability, they also demand exceptional social and emotional skills. To do these jobs well, employees must manage the uncertainty of working in a new discipline, use their judgment to make complex decisions, and work with others to achieve outcomes.

While technological advancements will create new roles, they are also changing existing roles. By 2030, the World Economic Forum estimates that 50 percent of the tasks we undertake as part of our jobs will change because of automation. Technology will replace repetitive tasks, like balancing books and editing written documents. This will free employees' time to draw on their social skills to do the things technology can't, like responding to a problematic situation by empathizing with a customer or collaborating with diverse people teams in a remote setting. In short, as the demand for technical roles increases and technological advancements transform existing roles, employees will come under increasing pressure to develop the interpersonal skills needed to do the things that machines cannot.

Transformation 2: Diversification of Talent

The second transformation is learning to work with people who do not look, think, or act like you. As a result of the pandemic, many employees can and do work from anywhere. Companies like Facebook, Shopify, Siemens, and the State Bank of India made public announcements following the pandemic that they will make working from anywhere permanent.

The increase in remote work and changing demographics mean

that employees can no longer afford to only network and collaborate with people similar to them. Instead, we must learn how to work with anyone. In addition, in 2020, the population of multiracial and racial and ethnic minorities aged eighteen and under exceeded those of white people. As a result, by 2044, more than half of all Americans will belong to a minority group (any group other than non-Hispanic white alone).

Working with people who may view or approach work differently can create conflict, which is great for innovation but can make collaborating difficult. To work on diverse teams requires the ability to bridge your differences with others—that is, you need exceptional social and emotional skills. Between 2016 and 2030, demand for employees to demonstrate social and emotional skills will grow across all industries. In the United States, this demand is expected to grow by 26 percent and in Europe by 22 percent for both technical and nontechnical roles.

Diversity is here to stay. As a result, the rapid diversification of workplaces will require us to increase our ability to regulate our emotions and behavior, collaborate with others, build relationships, and communicate effectively.

Transformation 3: Navigating Hybrid Workplaces
The third transformation most of us will encounter or have already encountered is learning to collaborate in hybrid workplaces—which include organizations where employees spend some time working in the office and some time working from home. In 2020, the consulting firm Deloitte found of the 1,500 companies it surveyed, 94 percent agreed that responsiveness and collaboration are critical to their organization's success today and in the future. Yet only 6 percent

of these companies believed their employees were responsive and collaborative. Companies that outcompete their peers can do so because they have built a culture where employees informally network, share information transparently, and work with anyone to get the job done. Who you work *for* will become far less important than who you work *with*. But how do you form bonds with team members you might never meet? How do you collaborate, innovate, and problem-solve in a digital workplace?

We know that hybrid working is overwhelmingly popular. More and more companies are allowing employees to work from home (WFH) permanently. During the pandemic and beyond, there has been a growing debate about the benefits and costs associated with WFH, but whether we like it or not, WFH is here to stay. A 2021 McKinsey survey of one hundred executives across industries and geographies found nine out of ten organizations plan to engage in hybrid working, a combination of remote and on-site work.

The rise of hybrid working has increased productivity as working from home provides fewer distractions and reduced commuting time. Furthermore, WFH offers increased flexibility, facilitating the retention of people from typically underrepresented groups, like working mothers, who often shoulder a disproportionate share of family duties, or people with physical disabilities, who may have difficulty navigating inaccessible public transportation or buildings.

Despite these benefits, there are many hidden costs associated with WFH, which we need to understand because they negatively impact our well-being and effectiveness at work. I want to be clear that I am not against WFH; I enjoy walking my kids to school instead of commuting to work each day. But I know it is essential to acknowledge the challenges that WFH will create for my career so I can manage them.

A global study conducted in 2021 found that isolation is the leading factor that worsened for employees working from home in all ten countries surveyed. Humans need to socialize. Loneliness was an issue before the pandemic, and it has accelerated with the rise of virtual work. The new world of work requires that employees work better together, yet the hybrid approach erodes our ability to do just that. Zoom simply cannot replace the connections people form in face-to-face meetings. The same research study also found that employees who work from home felt that decisions happen more slowly and that they are less clear about their responsibilities. They also found they had to work longer to achieve the same outcomes, negatively impacting their work-life balance. Working from home increases ambiguity.

The virtual work environment enhances the likelihood of miscommunication, misunderstanding, and disconnection. In a 2021 survey of nearly five thousand employees, McKinsey found that working from home during the pandemic increased fatigue, disconnection, and the deterioration of social networks, which reduced feelings of belonging at work. Despite the plethora of virtual tools of communication and collaboration connecting us to our colleagues 24/7 (like Zoom, Microsoft Teams, Slack, Dropbox, Google Drive, Skype, Periscope, Webex, and GroupMe), we are more disconnected than we were before the pandemic. Collaboration became harder virtually, and interactions became increasingly siloed. Hybrid work makes it harder to work together, which is bad for business.

A 2020 Boston Consulting Group survey of twelve thousand participants determined that employees satisfied with their social connectivity are two to three times more likely to be productive on collaborative tasks than those who were dissatisfied. Unfortunately, employees don't have the same opportunities in the physical workplace for spontaneous connection, like stopping by a coworker's desk for a chat or discussing weekend events in the communal office kitchen. While working from home has reduced commuting times and increased flexible working arrangements, the lack of social contact with coworkers deteriorates our mental health, which is terrible for productivity. During the pandemic, mental health issues and burnout increased; both are symptoms of declining informal and intimate human connections forged at the watercooler. Every one of us will face the challenge of finding new ways to connect, socialize, and collaborate in the new hybrid world of work, where it is challenging to do any of these things.

Hybrid work has raised the stakes on the need for teamwork while simultaneously making it more challenging to work together. Navigating our physical and digital workplaces means developing advanced social and emotional skills to juggle these different work environments, getting comfortable with managing ambiguity, and understanding how to adapt our work styles to meet the diverse needs of the people we work with.

In short, we need to learn how to manage how work gets done—regardless of where that happens or who it happens with.

Transformation 4: Learning to Manage the Informal

Finally, as these three changes—the increased demand for technical, social, and emotional skills, the diversification of organizations, and the need to collaborate in hybrid environments—transform how we work, the structure of organizations is also changing. The future workplace is where a virtual and physical informal network of diverse employees replaces the old hierarchy. Only 14 percent of executives believe that the traditional organizational structure makes their workplace effective with hierarchical job levels. Companies are now pushing for more agile, informal teams and structures to enable information sharing and collaboration to get the job done. To adapt to the technological changes underway, businesses need to become more responsive, including having less hierarchy to ensure faster decision-making and enable on-the-job learning and collaborative problem-solving. The 2018 study *Exploring the Future of Work: Results of the Futures Forum Study*, which examined expert opinions on the future of work, found that there will be less need for midlevel managers over the next ten years.

Workplaces will become more agile, so how we work will become less formal, organized, and clear-cut. The fourth fundamental change most of us will encounter is managing the informal aspects of work. Managing ambiguity—whether sensing when a presentation has gone on too long or understanding the subtext of what someone is saying—will become a fundamental skill. Employees will have to manage themselves, make decisions through consensus, and navigate the how of work to succeed. The new world of work is a "hypersocial workplace" because it requires one crucial skill: *the ability to read the people you work with*. If the rules are cocreated, we all have a role in shaping them. The challenge is that most of us don't know how to do this or are unaware of it.

Given the critical need to manage ambiguity, it makes sense that research finds people who have positive attitudes toward uncertainty and embrace the informal are more creative, perform to a higher standard, and make for better leaders. Biologically, our species' survival depends on our ability to adapt, manage uncertainty, navigate informality, and work with a range of different people—all of which require the ability to read the air. Unfortunately, there is just one problem . . . Our ability to manage ambiguity is decreasing at a time when workplaces are becoming more informal, resulting in what I call the *ambiguity paradox.*

Managing ambiguity involves several abilities, including solving problems that don't have a clear-cut solution, working on complex tasks with a high degree of novelty, and planning and creative thinking on the fly. Unfortunately, a 2019 study found that 70 percent of the eight hundred respondents aged twenty-four to thirty-seven scored below average on their ability to grapple with ambiguity. In addition, respondents aged eighteen to thirty-seven were twice as likely to score at the bottom 10 percent for their ability to manage ambiguity.

With this study in mind, it's notable that millennials—broadly speaking—when doing their job, want to avoid doubt and vagueness at all costs. Unlike previous generations, millennials excessively and continuously seek guidance and direction, which indicates they want to understand how others perceive them—they don't know how. As a result, organizations need to give millennials the tools to manage ambiguity, which includes helping them understand how to do their job without having all the information, responding to constant changes at work, and learning how to adapt their communication style to connect with different people. Millennials will soon make up most of the workforce. Businesses can enable this generation to manage ambiguity by learning to read the air and manage the how of work.

Like the monk in the old Zen story, the changes we are waiting for have come—but we need to wake up to the fact that we are on the other side. Our hybrid workplaces will increasingly consist of people who don't look or think like one another. We will need more advanced social and emotional skills to effectively collaborate, innovate, and solve problems to manage the inevitable technological advancements. The formality, clarity, and consistency of how, when, and where we work have given way to ambiguity, uncertainty, and informality. The case is clear: to navigate the new normal, we must master the informal.

Why You Read the Air

For my PhD, I conducted seventy-two interviews with men and women from two companies. About halfway through the process, I noticed that many participants didn't understand why they had to read the air. These participants would argue that reading the air felt like a waste of time. Surely, it's more effective to say exactly what you mean? Why can't everyone just be themselves regardless? Whenever people ask me these questions, I always respond by sharing a well-known story about the anthropologist Margaret Mead—first detailed in the book *The Best Care Possible* by physician Dr. Ira Byock. Many years ago, a student asked Mead if she knew what the first sign was that a culture had become civilized. Mead said when a femur (thigh bone) had been broken and healed, because if you break your leg in the animal kingdom, you cannot defend yourself, hunt for food, and find water, which means you will likely die.

However, when a broken femur has healed, it is evidence someone has taken the time to care for the injured person—by providing food, water, and safety. Mead argued that helping and caring for another person is where civilization starts.

Some historians debate whether or not this story is genuine or accurate, but I think these arguments miss the essential truth behind it. Our shared humanity is created from our capacity to care for one another. We find meaning at work through the connections we have with our coworkers, customers, and communities. Caring is how we connect; it's what makes us human. And reading the air is how we demonstrate care for one another, because it's how we manage the impact that our words and behaviors have on the people we work with.

Think about the Japanese businessman's failure to read the air. What was the impact on him? At best, he had irritated the client for exceeding their allotted time. At worst, he had lost a valuable business client and all the benefits that come with influential relationships. Relationships are valuable. Your ability to access informal networks, information, development, and advancement opportunities comes about through the connections you build and maintain at work—which academics refer to as *social capital*. Building social capital is one thing, but what we do with this social capital matters most.

Plenty of books, research studies, and academic journal articles make a case for learning how to manage office politics and influence, persuade, and even manipulate people to build the social capital you need to get ahead. I've read them all and realized that these approaches have one thing in common: they are entirely self-serving. As employees, we are encouraged to schmooze up to clients. Get your boss onside. Learn to play the game to get ahead. This old-fashioned belief in how to play the company game exists because most companies, education systems, media, and even leaders continue to perpetuate the myth that capitalism is a zero-sum game. To win it, we need to make money at all costs. Big business is built on greed, selfishness, and corruption. Companies maximize profits by exploiting employees, consumers, and the environment. While this approach might have tangible short-term gains, it's unsustainable. The push for profits over people and the planet creates enormous economic inequality leading to the loss of human rights.

What's bad for people and the planet is ultimately bad for profits.

A 2019 research study by *Harvard Business Review* found that sustainable businesses see more significant financial gains than their unsustainable counterparts. The fact of the matter is the world—and the world of work—has changed. Today's consumers and employees want companies to do better. The 2015 Nielsen Global Corporate Sustainability Report found that 66 percent of global consumers are willing to pay more for sustainable brands, and this number of consumers is increasing annually. Customers want to buy from businesses that practice equity and sustainability for the environment, economy, and society. A 2021 study examining over 2,500 people's work experiences, published in a *Harvard Business Review* article titled "What Your Future Employees Want Most," found that 86 percent of American employees want to work for a company that prioritizes "outcomes over output." Employees want employers to focus on *how the work gets done* by managing their organization's impact on customers, communities, and the environment.

In the new world of work, we need a new definition of what it means to win.

Managing the *how* of work is no longer a "nice to have." It is a business imperative. For businesses to survive on the other side, they need a new definition of what it means to win. If they hope to survive this sea change, companies need to change their focus from *what* gets done to *how* it gets done. The same is true for employees. We can no longer afford to believe that to survive the dog-eat-dog world of corporate bureaucracy we need to coerce, control, and persuade others to get them to do what we want them to do—even if it isn't in their own best interests.

How you earn social capital is just as important as how you spend it. Reading the air is how we manage ambiguity and informality and collaborate to achieve outcomes in a way that benefits everyone. A

2014 research study published in the *Leadership & Organization Development Journal* found that helping behaviors, like offering to support a colleague with their development or workload directly or indirectly, increase individual and team performance. One of the key findings of this study was that how much we feel like we belong determines our behaviors, the extent to which we help others, and, therefore, our overall performance. Paying it forward demonstrates that you value your coworkers because you care about their well-being.

Learning to read the air won't just advance your career; it will help you manage how you work to benefit the people you work with. You will discover how to connect with the people you work with, understand how they are wired, and utilize the information learned to help them advance in their careers. Importantly, you will understand why reading the air benefits your peers as much as it does you. The most influential person in any organization is the person who knows how to "read the air" because, with this knowledge, a person can make their entire organization work to benefit themselves, their colleagues, their customers, and their community.

The Four Practices for Managing How We Work

The future is here, but what each of us does with this knowledge determines if we will survive and thrive in the decades to come. How can I be so sure of this? Looking back at the history of how organizations and jobs have changed over the past century provides clues as to how they are likely to change in the future. Consider, for example, the introduction of ATMs into the United States beginning in 1985. There was significant concern that human tellers would become obsolete; if machines could dish out cash and take deposits, why would any bank need to hire humans to do it? While ATMs made it possible to operate banks 24/7 and with fewer employees, the initial cost savings encouraged banks to open more branches, which led to an increase in the number of tellers. ATMs did not replace bank tellers; they changed what bank tellers did. ATMs might be more accurate at counting and sorting cash, but they cannot manage customer queries, concerns, frustrations, and complaints. In short, tellers *serviced*.

The introduction of ATMs into the banking industry did displace some workers, but eventually, the technology was a net creator of jobs. Even with all the technological advancements coming our way in the next ten years, research conducted in 2021 examining how employment and skills will change by 2030 found that only 6 percent of companies expect their workforce in Europe and the United States to shrink because of automation and AI. About 77 percent of businesses expect no change, and about 17 percent expect their workforce to grow. While technology will replace routine, mundane tasks, it will also create new jobs and free us to cultivate and use more human skills, like creativity and interpersonal connection. To succeed in the new technological era, humans need to become more human—that is, do the things machines cannot, like managing informal systems by using empathy to console a customer whose card got swallowed by the ATM.

While observation might have worked in the past, it requires one thing we no longer have—time. The future is upon us, and we need a faster way to learn and absorb shared norms, or we risk being left behind. A 2008 research study by the consulting firm Catalyst finds that the number one thing employees wish they had known earlier in their careers was that it is not enough to work hard to succeed. You need to understand the informal aspects of working life to get ahead.

Approximately 78 percent of participants wanted their companies to provide them with the programs and practices needed to read the air. A 2010 study by Catalyst found that understanding shared norms plays a significant role in career advancement regardless of a person's gender, race, or ethnicity.

Japanese culture teaches people to read the air by observing and interacting with others. Developing the ability to read the air is strongly encouraged in Japan. There is even a video game about it— Nintendo Switch released the game *Kuukiyomi: Consider It*, where players are put in one hundred different situations and scored on how well they read the air. The same process of learning to read the air happens in organizations. No matter where you are in your career journey, it's not too late to learn how to read the air. Reading the air is a learned, or plastic, ability. It requires learning how workplaces work so that you can use your social and emotional skills to collaborate across differences, manage ambiguity, and work effectively in the hybrid world of work.

The new workforce is tired of game-playing and dog-eat-dog, and it has grown fed up with ambiguity, which is why the skill of reading the air is a timely, provocative, and proven success principle. We need to make the invisible practices visible. Our careers and workplaces depend on it.

When it comes to working life, what you see is not always what you get. The work world is a minefield of informal systems, like informal networks, information sharing, development opportunities, and advancement. To navigate these informal systems, you must learn to read your workplace and the people you work with, including yourself. When you know to read the air, your work is not about the work anymore; it's about influence. People won't see you as an employee who works long hours, always agrees with the leadership, or dots the i's and crosses the t's in lengthy reports. They'll see you as the employee who contributes value because you know what the company *really* wants and possess the "informal" skills needed to get there. You see what others don't. Most important, you know that no matter what upending event, like a global recession or pandemic, comes next, the formal systems will not be there to support you. But the air will always be there, and you'll know how to read it!

As an academic researcher, I love anecdotes (including stories like the Japanese businessman's), but empirical evidence is what I crave even more. Is the air "real"? What does the air look like? What is it comprised of? How do we learn to read it, and how can doing so serve to benefit not only me but also the people I work with?

This book is composed of twenty years of my research, including a review of more than three thousand academic journal articles, seventy-two original interviews with executives from two different organizations (in England and Australia), transcription of more than 110 hours of my interviews, and my analysis of more than one hundred thousand pieces of text, as well as two surveys, on large multinational consulting firms, with over three thousand participants.

Based on all this research, I have come to understand that what separates high performers who rise through the ranks from everyone else is the ability to read and navigate the informal aspects of work rather than following the "formal" rules. These people succeed because to achieve anything at work, one must understand and function within the informal side of working life that exists just beneath the surface.

I focused on ticking all the boxes for my advancement in my career. For too long I thought playing the game meant doing a decent job. I focused on the *what* of work at the expense of the *how*. I followed the rules as they'd been communicated to me through company policies, employee handbooks, and formal processes. Get a degree, check. Network, check. Have a great résumé (whatever that means), check. Get another degree, and maybe another after that. Buy a power suit, work late, have a firm handshake, lean in, innovate, pivot, create habits, find my why, and work with difficult people.

Check, check, check.

But after twenty years of ticking all the boxes and getting nowhere, I sat back and observed the people who *did* get promoted, and I realized that they did not rely on explicit knowledge—like multiple degrees—to get ahead. Instead, they spent most of their time managing *how* their work got done.

Learning to read the air can be challenging because this information is hard to pin down. Yet, for many of us, playing the game is the only way we learn the game's rules. One of the reasons for this is that the informal is rooted in an organization's history, values, and norms. Unfortunately, for new hires, none of that information is written down. Nor is it communicated consistently or explicitly, so learning it is a tedious and, at times, embarrassing game of trial and error. However, the 2008 research study by Catalyst found that people learn the informal side of working life by observing how people interact, dress, communicate (both in writing and orally), and engage in nonverbal behaviors. In addition, some participants in this study shared how they built their knowledge and experience from previous roles to understand how the shared norms work in new jobs.

Anything we come to know can be classified into two types of knowledge: tacit or explicit. In the example of the Japanese businessman and his client, explicit knowledge would be learning how to read a watch face to tell the time, whereas tacit knowledge would be learning to read the client's face and body language to know that the meeting was over.

Explicit knowledge is anything we learn through formal means, like school or workplace training programs. This type of information is definitive, easily communicated, shared, copied, and transmitted. Explicit knowledge is often called the *know what* of work because it's everything we learn to know what to do at work.

Conversely, tacit knowledge is the *know how* of work—the knowledge we develop to learn how to do what we need to do at work. Over time, you acquire tacit knowledge through your relationships because it includes sharing privately held insights, feelings, and opinions about an organization's culture and values. Reading the air uses the tacit knowledge you develop at work to get your job done. It is the most powerful form of knowledge because it is difficult to articulate, share, and copy.

But corporations continue to brainwash people into believing they must follow the explicit formal rules, policies, practices, and reward structures to get promoted. When employees start their careers, they are often told to schmooze, show good judgment, read leadership books, and master social media marketing and personal branding. The new workforce is no longer buying into the promise of "If you do this, you'll get that. If you don't, you'll fail." Rather employees are calling workplaces out. My research has led me to understand that no matter how hard you might work on these skills, the effort is essentially a waste. This is because when we focus on achieving tangible outcomes to get ahead, it is at the expense of managing how we achieve those outcomes. *How we work enables what we achieve—the how is more important than the what.*

When we manage the how of work, we are aware of and know how to engage in the four informal systems that exist in every workplace—including informal networks, informal information sharing, informal development opportunities, and informal advancement. Learning to read the air is essentially learning how these four informal systems work. While companies may have formalized processes for networking, sharing information, or developing and advancing employees, what matters more are the informal systems that sit alongside these processes. For example, you can attend all the formal networking events your company hosts or meet all the requirements for a promotion, but this doesn't guarantee you will develop the connections and support you need to progress. Formal processes articulate a company standard, but informal processes are how a policy or process is experienced. Managing the how of work means understanding how to manage the behaviors, interactions, and experiences we all have when it comes to how we network, share information, develop, and advance at work.

Informal networks are the lifeblood of organizations; they include all the informal relationships (i.e., employee–anyone) you might develop at work. These relationships are not limited to the formalized company structure (i.e., employee–manager). Informal networks include people you regularly interact with or socialize with, and connections you believe are mutually beneficial. For example, suppose you want to gain support for a project, consensus on critical decisions, introductions to important people, and support for career advancement. In that case, you need to know how informal networks function and what to do to manage them. Without informal networks, receiving the information, advice, and support you need to advance at work is almost impossible. The challenge is (despite popular opinion) you don't create an informal network by going to formal events and exchanging business cards over a cocktail hour. Chapter three reveals for the first time what informal networks you need, how they work, and what you need to do to make them work for you.

The more informal connections you have, the more likely you will have access to information that is hard to come by at work. When you stop at the watercooler for a chat or take ten minutes before a Zoom call to check in with your coworkers, these moments allow people to share crucial informal information. This can include information like upcoming organizational changes, informal feedback on your work, or understanding different people's perspectives on work-related issues. Formal information contains things like policies, processes, handbooks, or employee newsletters. But informal information is any knowledge shared casually, like over virtual coffee or after-work drinks. We develop an understanding of our workplace, our colleagues, and ourselves through the informal information we can access. Without informal information, it's very difficult to know how others perceive your capability and what you need to do to get that next promotion. Chapter four reveals how you can access the three types of informal information everyone needs to progress at work.

Your ability to develop and learn new skills depends on how many powerful people are willing to invest their time and energy in your career. The informal connections you develop give you access to development opportunities and the coaching and guidance needed to succeed in those opportunities. Most companies do not have a formalized process for deciding who gets the next short-term assignment, job rotation, high-profile project, or international assignment. Most of the time, managers rely on informal word-of-mouth recommendations when deciding who gets access to development opportunities. We need development opportunities to develop new skills and demonstrate what we are capable of. Most of us want to develop new skills and grow our careers. A lack of access to development opportunities is a key reason employees leave. A 2021 online survey conducted by Monster, the online recruitment company, finds that

45 percent of employees would leave their jobs because of a lack of access to development opportunities. Wanting development opportunities and knowing which ones are important and how to access them are different things. Chapter five will unveil which informal development opportunities are critical and how you can realize your potential and fulfillment at work.

While development opportunities are necessary to get promoted, they don't guarantee it. Advancement happens when the people making promotion decisions have a sense of who you are, what you value, and what it is like to work with you. Managing these perceptions requires an ability to "read the air" and "manage the air"—because you need to know how others perceive you and how to manage those perceptions. How would people describe what it's like to work with you? What are the people saying about you beyond your achievements? If all you have to do to get promoted is achieve outcomes without help from anyone or at the expense of other people's well-being, then only competent jerks would get the corner office. How you undertake your work matters as much as what you achieve. Your ability to work with others determines how willing people are to advocate for your career. In chapter six, you will discover what a career advocate is and how to find one so that you have the support you need to take on new challenges and have a meaningful career.

In a future rife with automation, artificial intelligence, virtual work, and increased demographic employee diversity, reading the air is how you navigate these changes. The 2017 Pearson report *Future of Skills: Employment in 2030* stated that social perceptiveness and coordination—the ability to read the air—will be the most critical skill needed in five to ten years. Technical skills (explicit knowledge) alone will not be enough to get that next promotion or make a meaningful contribution at work. The people who will successfully navigate the changes confronting most of us now are not focused on what's written. Instead, they know that the four informal systems that make up working life are just beneath the surface of the formal policies and processes. These individuals are not just aware of the informal systems; they know how to navigate them. They have learned to read the unwritten, informal, invisible "what a nice watch" rules—the air.

The new world of work requires a new way of working.

Whether it's a question of leading a remote team, earning a promotion in a world of cutbacks, branding yourself as a rising star, or getting your first job offer through Zoom, or if you are part of the new generation of corporate hopefuls who wonder: *How on earth do I get ahead?*, this book is your answer.

HOW WORK WORKS

1

A PLACE TO STAND

How to Belong

I will never forget my first day of primary school in South Africa. Looking out the window, I see a blur of green trees passing me by. I fantasize about jumping out of the moving pickup truck. That would be better than walking into an abyss of adolescent stares, snickers, and social isolation only the "outsiders" are privy to. Instead, I look out the passenger window and then down in dismay at my exposed legs. I tug at my skirt, wishing I were anyone other than a short girl with pale skin, glasses, braces, and a Harry Potter haircut. I want to look like everyone else, to disappear into the crowd. But instead, I am chauffeured to school by the automobile version of a social disease.

The pickup truck isn't exactly a pickup. For some unknown reason, everyone in my family calls it "the Kabal," and even though I don't know what Kabal means, it feels like the perfect name. The Kabal is one of a kind—an old, dented hybrid of a truck and pickup with the density of a tank. Like a giant character float at the Macy's Thanksgiving Day Parade, there is no way not to notice it. Paint cans, building equipment, and ladders hang off the back of the truck. They bang together with every pothole or hard brake the Kabal makes. The engine is loud, as it runs on diesel and tends to grunt and back-fire whenever it starts up. As we drive along, a trail of black smoke pours out of the exhaust attached to the roof, marking our path.

The school appears in the distance, and I feel my heart sink a little further. My dad insists he drop me off right outside the front entrance. There are no gates, just a large yard overflowing with teenagers. I struggle to crank the window handle of my dad's pickup. (The only way to open the door is from the outside.) As I roll down the window, I stretch my other arm out as far as possible to grab the outside door handle; a black BMW rolls up. A tall, tanned, blond-haired girl gets out. She shoots a braceless smile and waves to a cluster of more blond-haired girls staring at the Kabal and me.

The entire schoolyard is in a freeze-frame. Mouths are slightly open, with eyes even wider open. A loud bang makes everyone jump, and the blood drains from my body. The engine stops. My heart sinks; I know what this means. I put my schoolbag down on the curb and turn around. My dad gets out to grab his toolbox, and I climb back up into the truck to help him. I keep my back to the playground the whole time, believing that if I can't see them, somehow they won't notice me. I pull the ripped leather passenger seat up so my dad can reach the engine tucked underneath. He revs the motor, and the air becomes thick with black smoke. The performance is in full swing. *Bam!* The Kabal backfires. *Bam!* Twice. *Bam!* A third time. *Maybe no one heard it?* I feel relief as the engine restarts. I climb out from the Kabal—my cheeks, neck, and chest patchy and red. I pick up my schoolbag, head down, and make my way to the yard. Every kid's eyes meet mine as I look up, following me with a magnetic pull as I walk. Even my principal, Ms. Anderson, appears in the yard to look on. I hear whispers, giggling, and snickering. The kids step back when I pass, not wanting me to get too close. All my differences are laid bare, on display for everyone to see. As I walk across the playground, my eyes search for somewhere to stand. As I pass Ms. Anderson, she whispers, "Head up, King."

Most of us have a Kabal story. When accepted and included in a group, we feel secure, sure of ourselves, valued, and connected to others. But similarly, almost all of us can recall the acute pain that comes from being left out and excluded. The need to belong is universal, so it is painful when we feel we don't. I wanted more than anything to do what Ms. Anderson told me to do. How could I not let the bullying, isolation, and mocking get to me? I couldn't escape it. I couldn't find a place to stand during break time. I wasn't wanted anywhere. Not having a place to stand reminded me that I didn't belong, so I ate my lunch alone in the bathroom.

Belonging is feeling connected to your environment and the people in it.

As humans, our longing to belong has helped us survive. The belonging hypothesis, developed by researchers Roy Baumeister and Mark Leary in 1995, states that humans have a universal need to form and maintain at least some interpersonal relationships with other humans. Anthropological studies consistently find that people in all societies naturally form social groups. The process of natural selection favored people who could establish and maintain interpersonal connections with social groups. Being included in social groups was critical to gaining support, protection, and nurturing. Our ability to bond, collaborate, and cooperate across our differences enabled our species to reproduce and evolve.

Neurologists have found evidence that belonging is hardwired into our brains. Bonding and social interaction stimulate dopamine, the feel-good chemical. When we have positive interactions with other people, it sends a message to our brains that bonding feels rewarding. Conversely, the part of our brain that registers physical pain (the anterior cingulate cortex) is activated when people exclude us from social groups. Research finds it is worse to be isolated and ostracized than to be overtly harassed—according to a 2014 Canadian study published in *Organization Science*. This finding is particularly concerning given that a survey by the consulting firm EY of 1,789 full-time employees in the United States found that 40 percent felt isolated at work. Isolation damages our mental, emotional, and physical well-being—we all need a place to stand.

It took me a long time to realize that everyone has a Kabal in their lives—the one thing that separates them from everyone else. Every one of us has something that makes us distinct from the people in our lives, which we often feel desperate to hide. This is especially true in the workplace. To belong at work is to feel like you have a place to stand, which means knowing that what makes us different is valued by both our coworkers and by the companies that hire us. We belong when we feel valued for who we are and connected to our work environment and its people.

The extent to which we feel like we belong—whether we can reveal our different identities and know how to value those of the people around us—determines our engagement, morale, and productivity. Research finds that it's no different at work. When employees feel a strong sense of belonging at work, they are six times more likely to bring their best selves to work and excel in their roles. An extensive 2019 *Harvard Business Review* study found employees who felt like they belong experienced a 56 percent increase in job performance and a 50 percent drop in turnover rate. Belonging is critical to individual career success and organizational productivity.

Something as simple as being ignored by your colleagues in the hallways can lead to a 25 percent decline in an individual's performance on a team project. This is particularly concerning given that isolation is becoming even more difficult to overcome in the new world of remote work. Loneliness and isolation are the most significant concerns remote workers have. They negatively impact remote workers' productivity and well-being and increase stress and poor decision-making. A lack of belonging also contributes to various psychological issues, including depression, anxiety, and loneliness. Loneliness can even limit our life expectancy: a 2015 study found that loneliness can increase mortality rates by 26 percent.

But the disconnection we are currently experiencing makes fulfilling our universal needs very difficult. A 2021 study examining the experiences of one thousand employees working in a hybrid environment found that 53 percent of remote workers are worried about being left out of in-person meetings. In addition, the hybrid workplace makes it harder for us to connect, increasing opportunities for disconnect, distrust, and misunderstandings, all of which erode belonging. In this new world of work, it seems most of us are either experiencing or contributing to other people's Kabal moments. *We simply don't know how to belong or how to make others feel like they do.*

The Five Myths of Belonging

To understand how to build belonging at work, we need to examine some of the common misunderstandings and beliefs we hold about what it means to belong. Based on my research, I have found five pervasive myths perpetuating the win-lose mentality in organizations today. Therefore, redefining how we work starts with exposing beliefs about work that serve to perpetuate the status quo.

Myth 1: Belonging Has Always Been Available to Everyone
The notion that we all have an opportunity to belong at work is a relatively new one. Throughout human history, work has required

some degree of organization. Moreover, how we work has had to adapt quickly (and significantly) in response to changes in our work environments. For example, during the Industrial Revolution, companies like Ford Motor Company created and implemented mass production and assembly lines. This new way of working created new rules for how people had to work together. Almost overnight, workplaces—including Ford's production plants—were transformed into a hierarchy of supervisors and managers. Employees were given very specific, limited, repetitive tasks, which they had to master quickly. Each job contributed in a particular way to the assembly of a product. To get ahead in this workplace, it wasn't enough to work hard because the hours and pace of work were standardized for everyone. Rather, employees had to learn how to climb the corporate ladder. This meant being productive *and* playing the political game.

Office politics includes the behaviors, norms, and day-to-day exchanges we participate in. Politics is how work gets done, and it can positively or negatively impact our experiences of work. Our sense of belonging and connection to the culture in our workplaces is created or eroded in the everyday interactions we experience, which are often political. Politics happens when the most qualified, capable candidates lose out on promotion in favor of the most popular (or most well-connected) candidate—when the best decision for the business isn't made because it threatens a leader's position or the bottom line. *If you think your workplace doesn't engage in office politics, you simply haven't seen it yet.*

The major problem with office politics is that it doesn't work for everyone because it is an outdated way of working that benefits some people at the expense of others. Workplace cultures have been created and maintained by white men for decades. People in positions of power deliberately created the political game to exclude anyone different from them in any way, shape, or form. For example, I once worked for the CEO of a large multinational company that created weird unwritten rules for how people should work—from what they wore to how they organized or decorated their desks—and he expected everyone to comply. He even asked a male colleague to leave a meeting because he wore tan-colored shoes. The human resources manager later told me that this colleague would never get promoted, even though he was a top performer—all because of the color of his shoes.

The political way of working encourages everyone to believe that winning is a solo sport—your success comes at a cost to the people you work with. Countless books and academic journal articles make a case for learning to win at all costs: play the game, manage office politics, influence, persuade, and even manipulate people to get ahead. Unfortunately, these approaches have one thing in common: they are inherently self-serving and keep us disconnected. Belonging happens when we feel valued for who we are by the people we work with. The dog-eat-dog philosophy of most workplaces erodes meaningful relationships. This belief is so widespread that a 2008 survey of 250 managers in the United Kingdom found that 90 percent believe political skill is required to succeed. While the link between political skill and career success is clear, there is a problem: office politics is a win-lose game.

My extensive research into office politics finds that even if women and nonwhite employees engage in office politics, they may not benefit from it in the same way that white men do. In research undertaken by Kate Davey in 2008, women described office politics as an informal system that *keeps power with those who have it while excluding those who don't.* Office politics is a white man's game. They ensure that not everyone can belong because some rules don't apply to all.

The challenge white men face now is that the world of work has irrevocably changed. Technological advancements demand more significant innovation and creativity, which can only come from harnessing the value of perspectives that differ from their own.

To harness the value of a diverse and inclusive workplace, companies need to create an environment where people feel comfortable being different. And if you want to keep your seat at the leadership table, you must ditch old-school office politics.

Myth 2: To Belong, You Need to Fit In

The first time I heard the term *belonging* used in a corporate setting, I was consulting with a multinational professional services firm. As part of my work, I presented my findings from a recent culture survey to an all-white, all-male leadership team.

"We need to make sure people feel like they fit in. We need to create a culture of belonging." This statement came from Steve, the most senior person at the table. I was confused. Did Steve really think *belonging* and *fitting in* were the same thing? So I pressed him a bit harder:

"What does a culture of belonging mean to you, Steve?"

He turned toward me. "Where everyone feels like they fit in and understands the rules of the game," he replied.

Steve couldn't have been more wrong. He had made this comment in response to data I had presented, which found that over 92 percent of employees at his company believed that to get promoted and lead they needed to be dominant, assertive, aggressive, competitive, and willing to work long hours—just like all the white men in the room. Employees didn't feel they could speak up, meaningfully contribute, or share their identities and other lived experiences.

Steve didn't have a culture of belonging. He had a culture of "othering." His workplace valued one way of working, one way of thinking, and one way of behaving. Anyone who differed from this standard was "othered," treated as inferior and excluded. Soft-spoken individuals were passed over for promotions. Parents who couldn't work excessive overtime were overlooked for high-profile projects. Unlike Steve and the other men at that table, employees who were visibly different from them were less likely to advance, be allowed to contribute, or otherwise feel included.

Steve believed that belonging is synonymous with fitting in when the two couldn't be more different. We *fit in* when we hide or minimize our differences to be seen as similar to the dominant group as possible. Fitting in is simply learning to mesh with people who look, think, and act like you to the exclusion of everyone else, which is why Steve's leadership team was made up of people who look just like him.

His misguided belief highlights the paradoxical tension we all face when it comes to belonging: we want to be a part of a group and, at the same time, be ourselves. *Real belonging is only achieved when the very things that make us unique are also valued by the groups we are a part of.* Belonging is being accepted and appreciated for your Kabal rather than having to hide it to be seen as the same as everyone else.

As I explained to Steve, the pressure to fit in erodes belonging. Too often, consciously or not, we work harder to *bond* with people who share our similarities rather than challenge ourselves to learn to *bridge* our differences with people who don't. This creates "othering" workplace cultures that separate, isolate, and overlook people who differ from the dominant group.

Furthermore, sameness literally costs us. A 2019 research study published in the *Journal of Vocational Behavior* examined Black women's experiences of working in white male-dominated environments.

The study found that Black women often do not feel that their whole selves are valued or included at work, and they manage their identities by trying to hide or change how they present themselves at work to fit in. Black women find fitting in mentally and emotionally draining. The effort they have to put into concealing themselves stifles their creativity and innovation.

Employees who feel pressured to hide what makes them unique often experience poor psychological well-being. After all, it takes a lot of effort to hide who you are. We all want to feel included at work, but we want to do so while feeling like we can be ourselves. To reap the benefits of diversity, we must value people's differences. When we assign people an insider or outsider status and only invest our time to get to know people like us, we other everyone else—to our detriment. Othering makes it extremely hard for people in dominant groups to understand differences and different experiences of working life. Like Steve, many leaders I have met believe that they want to create a culture of belonging at work, but they don't realize belonging starts at the top.

To create a culture of belonging, leaders like Steve need to learn how to bridge their differences—especially with coworkers who are not represented at the leadership table. Ultimately, doing so will benefit Steve and the company as a whole. A 2020 research study by the consulting firm Glint found that when employees feel a strong sense of belonging at work, they are six times more likely to bring their best selves to the table and do their best work.

The challenge lies in the fact that employees in increasingly diverse workplaces face one disruptive change after another due to the pandemic, and leaders do not know what they need to do to create a culture of belonging. While most of us might not know how to belong at work, many of us know how to change ourselves to fit in. But hiding your differences to fit in is exhausting and pointless.

The Kabal was a daily, painful reminder to everyone, especially me, that I didn't belong. So I thought that if I begged my dad enough, he would let me walk to school and that somehow this would erase the Kabal from everyone's memory. But every morning, he drove me to school. And every morning, Ms. Anderson would watch over me as I walked across the yard as a reminder to hold my head up, which meant confronting and embracing what made me different.

To build belonging, focus on fostering and rewarding people's differences rather than their sameness.

Myth 3: Belonging Means Having a Specific Group of People to Belong To

It might seem counterintuitive at first, but research has shown that we build our sense of self when we feel part of a group. The memories, values, and ideas you have about yourself are created from interactions and experiences shared with other people. For example, a 2019 research study examining employees' experiences of not belonging at work found that losing their sense of self is the number one cost participants face. Participants in this study blamed themselves for not belonging at work, which negatively impacted their confidence and ability to do their jobs.

The fact is that every single one of us is a product of our relationships. Therefore, your sense of not belonging to a group will impact how you see yourself and perform. For example, when you don't feel like you belong at work, you are much more likely to hide your identity and struggle to form positive relationships and feel valued for what you do.

A lack of belonging has broader business implications, as well. Employees who feel othered or "outside" find it harder to collaborate, which is bad for business. A study published in 2004 in *Studies in the Education of Adults* finds that employees cannot learn or perform well in their jobs without some degree of belonging. There is a strong correlation between employees feeling accepted and willing to cooperate toward a collective goal. It isn't easy to voice your ideas, experiences, or perspectives when you don't feel like you belong. We lose ourselves when we change who we are to fit into the dominant norms and power structures at work by modeling other people's behaviors or changing how we dress and speak. Social exclusion and conformity go hand in hand.

Zola, the only Black girl in my year at primary school, showed me early on that *belonging isn't about feeling like you are a part of a specific group; instead, it is about feeling like you can be yourself regardless of your group.*

I went to school during apartheid. Zola was one of the first Black students to join my year. Despite being one of the only racial minority students, Zola knew how to belong. She was a scholarship student who always smiled and got along with everyone. At lunchtime, she would play hacky sack on the playground with different groups of friends and sometimes even on her own.

Often, when I would make my way to the bathroom to eat my lunch, Zola would stop me and encourage me to join her on the playground.

One day after school, a barefoot Zola walked past me as I waited for the Kabal to arrive. "Where are your shoes?" I asked.

"I don't want to ruin them," she replied. "I have a long way to walk; this is my only pair."

As I got into the Kabal, I asked my dad to pull over when we passed Zola so we could offer her a ride home. She smiled and thanked me profusely as she climbed into the Kabal. My cheeks burned with shame for ever feeling embarrassed about my ride.

Myth 4: As Companies Become More Diverse, They Also Become More Inclusive

While companies are becoming more diverse—in terms of demographic representation—they are also becoming less inclusive. Even as more nonwhite, non–cismale employees enter the workforce, those same employees feel marginalized and devalued. This phenomenon is known as the *diversity paradox*.

This paradox exists because most workplaces do not value difference; they tolerate it. For example, hiring underrepresented employees into an organization might demonstrate that your company welcomes diversity, but welcoming is not the same as valuing.

When organizations value difference, employees feel they can be themselves precisely because they know their organization wants their unique contribution. The 2020 McKinsey *Diversity Wins: How Inclusion Matters* report, which surveyed over one thousand companies across fifteen countries, found that 52 percent of respondents felt optimistic about diversity, while only 31 percent felt negative. However, only 29 percent of respondents felt optimistic about inclusion, while 61 percent of those surveyed felt negative. Diversity without inclusion costs businesses. Employees who don't feel included are more likely to feel disengaged and quit. In addition, a Gallup study found that when employees are excluded from their colleagues, it reduces productivity, which is estimated to cost the US economy between $450 and $550 billion per year.

The fears most of us experience regarding job uncertainty, economic downturns, or technological advancements make our need to feel included even more critical. Our comfort in sharing the different aspects of who we are at work determines our engagement, morale, and productivity. But it's hard to share your ideas when you are worried your colleagues are too busy judging how you speak rather than paying attention to what you're actually saying.

Bringing diverse talent into an organization is one thing, but it is quite another thing to value that talent.

Despite wanting to feel connected, employees often experience isolation or exclusion from informal social groups at work, which is alarming given that today we spend more time working than at any other point in human history. The average American workweek has risen from about thirty-five hours in 1930 to a standard forty today, and many people log more hours than that: workers in full-time jobs in the United States worked just over 9.3 hours on an average weekday in 2017. As working hours have increased, so, too, has the importance of working relationships, which now provide the support many colleagues used to get from their families and the broader community. Moreover, as we spend more time at work, we want more personal satisfaction and fulfillment from our jobs, and we get this when we feel a sense of belonging.

As a workplace culture expert, I don't focus solely on diversity or inclusion when working with companies. Diversity and inclusion are not the problems we are trying to solve. You can work in a company with a high degree of demographic diversity and still have employees who do not feel included. You can have an inclusive workplace where employees feel comfortable speaking up, engaging in disagreements, or sharing ideas, but the organization lacks demographic diversity. Realizing a diverse, equitable, and inclusive workplace happens when we all know how to create a workplace that values all employees' differences—a workplace where anyone can belong.

Building belonging at work starts with learning how to value difference.

Myth 5: You Don't Need to Belong to Get Ahead

It was a cold autumn morning as I looked around the playground at students standing in straight lines with almost military precision. Uniformed and groomed to perfection, a sea of students stood in silence, waiting to hear who had been made a prefect, the equivalent of a class president in America.

To be named a prefect was no small feat. Every year students and teachers would nominate candidates based on who best represented the school's values. The final candidates were then voted into their position by both the student body and the faculty. Prefect selection was more than just a popularity contest; students had to demonstrate that they had gone above and beyond to personify the school's ethos. Becoming a prefect was a profound public statement of a student's character and a huge personal achievement.

Of course, I wanted to be a prefect. Badly. I was in my final year of primary school; this was my year to be a prefect. But getting it or not wouldn't define me. I no longer sat in the bathroom at lunch. I was friendly to everyone—even the kids who teased me. I helped at the school food shop during recess and went to the library whenever possible. I began to engage a bit more in my schoolwork and even discovered that I liked English and science. I looked after the younger, smaller kids on the playground at lunchtime to ensure they were not alone. The greatest gift being an outsider gave me was the ability to discover how to be myself and permit others to do the same. I gradually found a place to stand.

The teachers began to assemble at the front of the lineup, but every student's eyes were on Ms. Anderson. Early morning condensation formed a cloud of mist around her, amplifying her presence. She coughed to clear her throat and then said, "We will announce this year's prefects. Congratulations to everyone who was nomi-

nated." We held our collective breath and leaned forward in antic-
ipation.

"Adele Smith, congratulations! You have been selected as prefect for your year. Please come forward to accept your pin." *Okay*, I
thought. *One down, two to go. There is no chance it can be me—the Kabal girl—so let's get it over with.*

"Stephen Laurie! Congratulations, you have been selected as prefect for your year. Please come forward to accept your pin.

"And . . . Michelle King—"

My heart stopped. There was a gasp in the crowd. Another girl
in my year called Michelle stepped forward only to be pulled back
by the student standing next to her, who whispered gently, "It's not
you." And then that same student turned and pointed directly at me
and said, "It's her."

I still didn't register what was happening until Ms. Anderson
looked at me, nodded her head in encouragement, and repeated my
name.

"Michelle King."

A sea of heads turned to look at me while my whole face and neck
burned bright red. But I didn't feel the need to disappear for the first
time. Instead, I straightened my glasses and lifted my head up to look
at Ms. Anderson as I walked to the front. Ms. Anderson pinned my
prefect badge onto my blazer and winked at me while she whispered,
"Don't ever forget, King—*head up.*"

To belong is to climb out of a Kabal and walk through the smoke
onto your schoolyard with your shoulders back and head held high
because you know that belonging is forged through the value we give
to the things that make us unique.

*To belong is to know that what you value about yourself is also valued
by the people you work with.*

When we don't feel like we belong at work, we leave. Since April 2021, approximately nineteen million American workers (and counting) have left their jobs. This mass exodus is not limited to one country or industry, either. A 2021 McKinsey study, which included 5,774 participants from Australia, Canada, Singapore, the United Kingdom, and the United States, found that 40 percent of employees stated they were somewhat likely to quit in the next three to six months. Approximately 36 percent of participants quit without having a next job lined up. The great resignation is likely to stay, as 63 percent of employers expect the problem to worsen or continue for the foreseeable future—but very few organizations can concretely say *why* their people are quitting.

Most employers in this study believed the top three reasons employees leave include issues with pay, work-life balance, and well-being. But employee feedback revealed that none of those issues cracked the top three most common reasons for resignation. Those top three reasons *did* include not feeling valued by the organization, not feeling valued by their manager, and not feeling a sense of belonging.

When we don't belong, we feel emotionally detached from our workplace and the people we share it with, making it easier to quit or disengage from our workplaces. A job becomes transactional— it's just a way to pay the bills. A 2020 research study titled *Fostering Workplace Belongingness Among Employees,* which included a survey of 390 participants, found that when participants felt emotionally attached to their workplace, they tended to feel more appreciated, recognized, and included in social interactions.

A person leaves a job mainly because of a lack of emotional attachment to the workplace—what researchers call "affective commitment." A 2017 article published in the *Review of Applied Psychology* found that when people feel connected and committed to their colleagues, they report higher levels of social support, increased performance in their tasks, lower stress levels, reduced emotional burnout, and increased fulfillment at work. We feel connected to the people we work with when we know that they value our differences.

You are more likely to feel safe, respected, and connected to your colleagues when you feel valued for who you are. The more you are included, the more likely you are to speak up, share your ideas, and contribute, which improves your performance. Belonging is a practice. It is something that we do to better relate to one another. It is also something we do to better understand who we are. In business, belonging is as important for individual success as it is for collective success. We thrive or quit depending on how much we feel we belong to a place and the people in it. We build a sense of self through our connections to other people, especially at work. Belonging happens when what we value about ourselves is valued by the people we work with.

Belonging: At the Heart of Reading the Air

Recently, I met with the board of a large global media company to discuss the cultural challenges they were facing—including low levels of employee retention, engagement, innovation, and collaboration.

Halfway through the meeting, Matthew, the company chairman, stood up, put his hands on the desk in front of him, turned to face the chief human resources officer, and said, "When will all this DEI [diversity, equity, and inclusion] stuff go away? I want to get back to business. I'm tired of distractions. I want to focus on what matters . . .

you know, real work." Matthew's question isn't unusual. A lot of people are tired of "DEI stuff."

Matthew didn't know it, but the reason his company can't solve the cultural challenges (which negatively impact the company's financial performance) is that he views DEI as separate from real work. Managing how your workplace works is at the heart of doing business.

I have spent two decades researching workplace cultures, including the behaviors, norms, and interactions we all engage in that make up our collective experience of working life. At the same time, I have worked with global companies of all sizes to build workplace cultures that enable every employee to feel valued for their unique talents, capabilities, and differences. I do this by spending a lot of time coaching and advising senior executives and board members responsible for building these cultures.

Over the two decades, I have witnessed DEI's increasing popularity. Companies in the United States spend around $8 billion annually on DEI initiatives. Yet, roughly every year, it is estimated that 40 percent of employees feel isolated and excluded. While there might be a genuine curiosity about DEI, that seems to be where the effort stops. The 2018 *State of Diversity Report* by the consulting firm Atlassian finds that employees were 50 percent less likely to participate in DEI initiatives than they were the year before. Employees are disengaged because they have become exhausted, disillusioned, and frustrated with all the DEI talk and no action.

Companies might be able to articulate why DEI is good for business, but how many leaders like Matthew have a personal case for change or know how to practice DEI in delivering their work? Without knowing why DEI matters to you, it's tough to believe it really matters to your business.

Cultures are not static; we create them daily through the behaviors and exchanges we engage in. If we don't know how to behave in a way that makes our colleagues feel like they belong, then they likely never will. Unsurprisingly, the consulting firm Deloitte surveyed 245 companies and found that 71 percent aspire to have an inclusive culture that improves business performance. Still, only 11 percent of these companies have this work environment. So the subtext of Matthew's question, which many people want to ask but are afraid to, is, *Why should I care about DEI?*

Companies need the collective power of many great minds to innovate, create, and problem-solve. But what makes great minds so great is that they don't all think alike. It is almost guaranteed that you will have to learn how to connect, understand, and work with people who do not look, feel, or act like you. In the United States, the Bureau of Labor Statistics forecasts that as early as 2024, there will be an increase in the diversity of employees across nearly all demographic categories, including age, race, ethnicity, and gender. Collaborating effectively with your teammates requires you to learn how to value difference—by making belonging a practice.

The new world of work requires a new way of working.

Whether we want to admit it or not, the new world of work requires that we work together to get ahead. Individual success (defined by simply achieving individual outcomes) cannot come at the expense of your colleagues. Excluding or using your teammates to get ahead will negatively impact your ability to do your job. While we might all have different ways of working, what connects us is our need to work together to achieve positive outcomes.

My research has found that people who feel connected to their colleagues achieve their career aspirations faster (and with more work-life balance) by managing how they informally network, share information, and access development and advancement opportunities. And they do this in a way that benefits them *and* their coworkers. Your ability to read the air will enable you to connect to your work environment and find a place to stand within it.

2

THE TRUST EXCHANGE

How to Read the Air

The degree to which we feel like we belong at work depends on the nature of our relationship with our workplace. We don't often think about our job as a relationship, but it is, at least in a sense. Your job is a reciprocal relationship. You exchange your time, energy, and expertise for money, advancement, and fulfillment at a basic level. The exchange can happen *only* if both parties trust each other, which is why I refer to the relationship between workplaces and employees as a *trust exchange*.

Trust can be difficult to define, but most of us can recall a time we worked with someone who didn't hold up their end of the bargain.

I saw a quote the other day by American business tycoon Warren Buffett that really summed this up; it read, "Trust is like the air we breathe. When it is present, nobody notices. When it is absent, everybody notices."

I have built and broken trust in workplaces. And I have had workplaces make and break my trust in them. Without trust, it is impossible to belong.

I experienced this firsthand when I secured a high-profile role working in human resources for a multinational tech company. This company was incredible, with some of the most talented people in my field on the payroll. They earned exorbitant salaries and had the best benefits and opportunities to advance. I lost count of those who said, "You are so lucky to work for them. I would kill to have that job."

I did feel lucky. It was the job of my dreams.

But soon after joining the company, I noticed that I had developed a constant feeling of unease. Everyone seemed to say and do the right thing, but there was something in the air that didn't *feel* right to me. In my first week with the company, one of my teammates was fired. We were told it was because she was underperforming. But over time, people shared that her performance was not the problem. She was let go because she was perceived as difficult for having raised her experiences of bullying and exclusion within the team. And then, every week after that, it seemed like someone else was terminated, with each departure announced publicly and abruptly.

Fired colleagues confided in me, sharing how they were encouraged to sign nondisclosure agreements, which initially didn't seem unusual. Every employee was provided with severance pay so long as they signed an agreement promising never to say anything disparaging about the company. But what made this practice weird was the amount of money people were paid. The company paid everyone severance pay, which totaled anywhere between six months to two years of a person's salary—regardless of how long they had worked at the company. The company was effectively buying people's silence no matter the cost or risk.

My earlier research taught me that to understand the culture of any workplace, look at how the people at the top of the ladder behave. Good leaders, after all, are supposed to set the standard for behavior and other expectations for all employees at every level. Unfortunately, the same is true for bad leaders. Our collective behaviors make up our lived experience of work—which is to say, the culture of a given workplace.

When it came to the leaders in my workplace, what I saw wasn't good. In my first week, I attended a leadership course off-site, which allowed me to spend time with managers from across the business. Unfortunately, they all seemed to behave similarly: gossiping, boasting, and self-promoting were normalized. However, in one-on-one exchanges, leaders admitted that they only engaged in these behaviors to make their achievements known, which they believed was necessary to keep their jobs.

This, I realized, was a culture of fear.

I coached and supported employees with different performance challenges as part of my job. As the weeks passed, the employees I worked with started to share accounts of racism, sexism, favoritism, and bullying—but no one ever felt safe enough to call these behaviors out or raise them with their line leader or HR.

As part of my induction, I met with Rachel, one of the executives I'd be supporting.

"You need to change what you are wearing; no one wears all black," she told me as I shook her hand. It was my first time meeting her. "So, what's your story?" she continued. "Why are you here?" I sat down and began to share my background but was quickly cut off. "No one cares about your qualifications or experience, honey. It's all about *results*."

Rachel didn't have follow-up questions for me, but she continued to interrupt me with barbed comments and sharp putdowns. Rachel covered all the bases. She criticized my handbag and the eccentricities of my accent. She downplayed my achievements and mocked my taste in shoes, where I lived, the school my kids went to, and the fact that my husband couldn't find a job. Rachel spoke a lot and never allowed me to finish my sentences. I started to fidget in my seat and glanced nervously at my watch, wishing for the meeting to be over.

Finally, I couldn't take it anymore, so I cobbled together a pitiful reason for leaving. I said something about having to go to the next meeting, but I was out of my seat and out the door before she could question it.

I walked into the nearest bathroom, shut the stall door, and cried. As I stood looking around the stall, I realized it reminded me of being back in primary school, wincing at the sight of the Kabal waiting for me outside the playground.

That was all within my first week on the job. As the months passed, Rachel started not inviting me to meetings and then pretended she had after the fact, which meant I looked like I was the one slacking off by not attending. She even started bad-mouthing me to my colleagues. On one particularly memorable occasion, I had dialed into a Zoom call early—my camera was off and muted—as we waited for our colleagues to join. Rachel must have thought her microphone was muted, as she was having a phone conversation with a colleague during which she called me various names and mocked how I dressed.

Embarrassed and ashamed, I plucked up the courage to tell my boss after the meeting. "How strange," she replied. "Rachel has only ever been nice to me. She is very senior. I hope you two can get along."

I felt completely invalidated. Over nine months, I would try to revisit the conversation with my boss. Whenever I shared my experience, she dismissed it, using twists of logic and magical excuses to try to make me feel like it had never happened. I started to think maybe she was right. I began to feel self-conscious about what I wore and how long I spoke in meetings. I even started saving and documenting emails to remind myself what meetings I had and had not been invited to. I questioned my judgment and capability. I slowly lost confidence in myself. I eventually stopped speaking up in meetings entirely. I stopped sharing ideas.

This continued until one day a colleague, James, pulled me aside and asked, "Michelle, what's happened to you? You didn't say anything in our last meeting, and I know you have some thoughts on what was discussed."

I took a breath, holding back tears. This was the moment I knew that I had to quit. If I couldn't be myself at work or be valued for that, this was not an environment where I could do a good job. I simply had no place to stand in this organization.

When I gave my notice, my boss had the audacity to act shocked.

"Why are you doing this? No one ever quits our company. You are making a big mistake." I didn't feel safe enough to tell her the truth: that she had broken my trust, and that wasn't something I could repair on my own or wanted to with her. I had shared my painful experiences of bullying on numerous occasions, and she had explicitly invalidated every single one of them.

As I worked out my two-week-notice period, I had to meet with Rachel one last time to do a handover. I was about to leave when Rachel said, "I will miss working with you, Michelle. I am sorry if I was difficult. The truth is, I just didn't think we needed someone at your level, but I guess we did. I know I behaved badly."

A week later, during my exit meeting with my boss, she also apologized. "I was gaslighting you. I knew she was bullying you; I just didn't want to do anything about it because she is so senior and it would make my life difficult. I'm sorry."

On my last day, the CEO sent me an email. Just one line that read, "I am sorry. We will do better."

Too little. Too late.

I moved on to my next job. Two months later, both Rachel and my boss were fired.

Rachel wasn't trustworthy because I couldn't trust the motivations behind her behavior. I couldn't predict why she was doing what she was doing. To be safe, I had to assume anything Rachel did was not in my best interests. There are numerous academic definitions of *trust*, but for me, each of these definitions can be boiled down to one thing—predictability. We trust people when their behavior is consistent and we can accurately predict why they behave the way they do. Understanding this makes it easier to predict how someone will behave in the future. We trust our workplaces and the people we work with when we know how they are likely to behave, and we believe they are acting with our best interests in mind. When you decide to join a company, there is uncertainty and risk involved in making the up-front commitment. You need to trust your hard work will be met with financial rewards and opportunities for promotion.

But the trust exchange does not involve *only* these tangible benefits; when we invest in a company, we also want to be met with approval, support, career fulfillment, meaning, and belonging. When we receive these intangible benefits, it is evident that your workplace is trustworthy, so you should continue investing your time in it. Trust begets trust.

Everyone needs to uphold their end of the bargain for the trust exchange to work. After all, trust is what links people to their environment and one another. So, for people to belong, they need to trust their workplace and the people they work with.

If you want to know whether you trust your workplace, take a moment to consider the following questions:

- Do you know how employees are expected to behave at work, and do these behaviors make you feel included, respected, and accepted for who you are?
- Do you feel comfortable freely expressing your feelings?

- Are disagreements in your organization discussed openly?
- Do you trust the competence and capability of the people you work with?
- Are you willing to voice your opinions, raise questions, and share your ideas?
- Do you feel you can be yourself rather than hiding or changing who you are to try and fit in at work?
- Do you feel included in informal social groups or networks at work?
- Do you feel you know what is going on at work and have access to the informal information you need to get your job done?
- Do you believe that your organization is committed to your development and that you can access opportunities to learn and grow?
- Do you believe your coworkers are willing to support and advocate for your career advancement?

You probably don't fully trust your workplace if you answered no to some or all of these questions. But, unfortunately, the bad news is a lot of people don't trust the people they work with. According to a 2020 Edelman survey of thirty-three thousand people in over twenty-eight countries, one in three people do not trust their employer.

A workplace that does not trust employees will likely have an overabundance of rules, policies, and procedures. Research has found that low levels of trust in workplaces increase bureaucracy and, in turn, limit employees' creativity, individual accountability, innovation, and proactivity. But a workplace that trusts its employees is likely to have fewer rules and policies. In a high-trust organization, employees are more likely to feel like they belong, which means they're more likely to share information, admit mistakes, collaborate effectively, and support one another's career ambitions.

Reading the air is how we build trust at work. Reading the air is necessary because workplaces are becoming less formalized and more democratic, requiring a high degree of trust to navigate. A 2017 study examining the future of work titled *Exploring the Future Workplace: Results of the Futures Forum Study* stated that increasingly, organizations are becoming self-managing, autonomous teams, and informal. Decision-making is becoming more decentralized. Importantly, individual performance is no longer determined by your achievements alone; instead, your performance will be assessed by your team. Your coworkers, rather than your manager, will review and collectively decide your annual performance rating. This assessment will be based on how well you can work with your coworkers, how much they trust you, and vice versa.

Trust and Hybrid Workplaces: The Missing Link

When trust is gone, everyone notices. Trust impacts all aspects of working life. Rachel broke my trust first, but I lost faith in my boss, the CEO, and coworkers. I no longer believed my workplace had my best interests in mind. Research has found that how much you trust the people you work with affects the quality of your relationships, which determines your sense of belonging, productivity, job satisfaction, and well-being. Trust enables what we do and how we do it.

Research has also examined the effects of trust and found that its presence leads to enhanced individual, team, and organizational performance. There is a range of beneficial outcomes when employees trust one another; according to a 2017 *Harvard Business Review* article, people who work for companies that trust their employees know how to collaborate, share ideas, support one another, and work together, which is why these organizations report:

- 74 percent less stress
- 40 percent less burnout
- 13 percent fewer sick days
- 106 percent more energy at work
- 76 percent more engagement
- 50 percent higher productivity
- 29 percent more satisfaction with their lives than employees working in low-trust environments

Based on this research, we also know that employees who trust their organizations the most have an average income 10.3 percent higher than those who only *somewhat* trust their organizations. Trust not only improves the potential earnings of an employee but it can also be fundamental to a company's functioning. A 2016 study by PricewaterhouseCoopers reported that 55 percent of CEOs think a lack of trust threatens their organization's growth.

The bottom line is that what we do and how we do it depends on how much we trust our workplaces and how much our workplaces trust us. Your relationship with your workplace is a reciprocal social contract, one that you both uphold by building trust.

Employees give up their time, energy, and capabilities in exchange for two types of rewards: extrinsic and intrinsic. Extrinsic rewards include things like bonuses or pay that are generally straightforward to fulfill. However, intrinsic rewards, which include how much employees trust their coworkers or feel like they belong, are much harder to realize because they are intangible. But in the long run, it is more important that your employer provides you with intrinsic rewards because they play a critical role in employee engagement, job satisfaction, and retention.

A 2019 research study by the consulting firm EY finds the top three reasons people feel like they belong include how much employees trust their workplace, whether employees feel like they can be themselves, speak up, and share information, and the extent to which employees feel like their contributions are valued. We might join our company for money, but we stay because we feel like we belong. People are 50 percent less likely to leave their workplace and 167 percent more likely to recommend their employer as a place to work if they feel like they belong—according to career and leadership coaching platform BetterUp's 2020 study, *The Value of Belonging at Work*. We join a workplace where we trust that giving our expertise and time will result in all the benefits listed in our employment contract, including our pay and benefits. The more we achieve, the more tangible benefits we hope to accrue, but eventually, there is a limit to what we can earn. At the end of the day, what keeps us attached to our workplaces is how much we feel like we belong.

Rachel had bullied me for months, and I'd told numerous people (like my boss and my boss's boss) about it. They should have intervened, but their failure to do so broke my trust, which made it impossible for me to feel like I belonged. And the less I felt like I could be myself and belong, the less I trusted the people I worked with to accept me for who I am. Trust determines the strength of our relationship with our workplace; when it breaks, we break away.

A 2019 research study published in the academic journal *Nonprofit Management and Leadership* found that when people are treated fairly, they are more likely to feel like they belong, which makes them believe their workplace is more trustworthy. The trust exchange is reciprocal because the extent to which you trust your workplace and your workplace trusts you determines your lived experience of the organization. For example, when a person bullies you at work, not only does this harm your relationship with that person, but how your workplace responds to you being bullied will make or break your relationship with your organization.

The everyday informal norms and behaviors employees engage in generate or dissolve trust because these behaviors tell us what people value—and what our workplace values. Trust is less likely to develop in workplace cultures that prioritize winning at all costs—according to a 2004 academic study published in *American Behavioral Scientist*. Winning-at-all-costs cultures value short-term results and individual achievement over sustainable solutions and collective well-being.

Mutual trust is far more likely to develop in cultures that value close relationships, cooperation, and reciprocity. A workplace that tolerates bullies like Rachel is a workplace that values a dog-eat-dog culture. You can't trust your coworkers in a workplace that does not value trust.

We need our workplaces to value trust. Businesses are facing unprecedented changes like globalization, increasing competition, technological advancements, and the diversification of customers and employees. Getting employees from different cultural backgrounds to work together, share information and expertise, and value one another's contributions requires a high degree of trust. However, a 2016 study by the consulting firm Edelman found that one in three employees does not trust their workplace. While these findings can't get much worse, today's hybrid workplace is even harder to build trust in. Research has found that certain conditions, like remote or hybrid working, make it more difficult for people to work together.

For example, it is more difficult for employees to build relationships virtually because there is less opportunity or time for employees to get to know one another by engaging in casual non-work-related conversations.

More important, virtual working limits our ability to pick up on social cues, like a person's facial expressions and tone of voice. These cues help us assess a person's trust, warmth, empathy, and interest. In a face-to-face situation—like a team meeting—it's much easier to make these assessments, ask personal questions, share non-work-related information, and ultimately bond. A 2005 academic study published in the journal *Strategic Change* examined trust in virtual teams and found that because virtual communication makes it harder to pick up on social cues, reading the air and building trust become much more difficult.

But as we look toward a future in which hybrid and even fully remote work is the norm and not the exception, we must learn to be more intentional about building trust.

How Workplaces Work: The Four Informal Systems That Matter Most

In the introduction of this book, I shared the four informal systems that make up our experience of working life: informal networks, informal information sharing, informal development, and informal advancement. In any work environment, these four informal systems matter most when it comes to the trust exchange because these four systems represent the things people want most when it comes to their working life. We want to feel like we belong, which can only happen if we are included in informal networks at work. We want to

understand our workplaces and how we can contribute, which requires that we have access to informal information. We also want to
know that our hard work will be met with access to informal development opportunities and support for our advancement.

Throughout my career, I have stumbled upon the four informal
systems and learned how to navigate them through trial and error. However, these experiences only made sense once I started researching the four informal systems that underpin how workplaces
work. One of these experiences happened early in my career when I
oversaw an executive committee (ExCo) meeting, an annual meeting of the company's most senior executives. My job was to support
the chief executive officer and chief human resources officer. As part
of my role, I managed all aspects of the ExCo meeting, including par-
ticipating in the session.

A month before that first ExCo meeting, I received a full briefing
from Jo, the chief human resources officer, whose job was to ensure
the entire two-day meeting event went off without a hitch. My boss
even gave me an A4 binder filled with notes detailing the process for
managing the event: in it were every attendee's airport pickup *and*
drop-off time, hotel confirmation, and meal preferences. Weeks of
preparation went into this event. As the host, I managed the meeting
agenda and content, logistics, catering, accommodation, and overall
experience. It was a highly sought-after development opportunity
because it came with the privilege of being in the room with some of
the company's top leaders.

I worked hard to prepare for the session and ensured I knew that
binder inside and out. I ticked off everything on the to-do list. Day
one went smoothly, and as the meeting ended, in front of all the ExCo
members, Jo asked, "Michelle, are you joining us at dinner?"

I panicked. I had not planned for this. "Apologies, no, I can't join you all," I replied, trying to bow out graciously. "I still must type up the minutes and prepare for tomorrow's agenda."

Jo nodded but pressed on. "It would be good, Michelle, if you could come to dinner; don't worry about the notes." I breathed a sigh of relief at her encouragement and went to dinner.

The next day I arrived well before the meeting started to type up the minutes, but I only managed to get halfway through. Based on Jo's words the day before, I assumed no one would call on me to present.

As everyone took their seats, Jo announced to the room:

"Michelle, please present the full actions and notes from yesterday's meeting on the screen, will you?"

I felt the blood drain from my face as the entire ExCo stopped what they were doing, turned, and looked at me. I stumbled through, red-faced and close to tears, presenting the half-finished notes and actions. With all eyes on me, I noticed some heads shaking and heard a few frustrated sighs. I knew that despite all my hard work, this would be my defining moment.

When Jo said *Don't worry about the notes*, she wanted me to understand that notes are not as important as getting to know the people in the room. Jo was indirectly telling me that I needed to treat my relationships with as much importance as I do my work, which means going to dinner. What good was it to do an excellent job if none of the ExCo members knew who I was? Jo still needed the notes, but she also wanted me to cash in on the reward of being able to network informally with the very people who could decide my next career move.

But I hadn't anticipated that I might be invited to dinner, and I didn't know how to make the most of that informal networking experience. Had I known how workplaces really work (the four informal systems that make up a given workplace), I would have known how crucial informal networking was and how to do it. I might have even anticipated that Jo would want me to go to dinner and prepared accordingly, or I would have suggested I attend dinner myself because I would have known how to read the air.

To read the air effectively, we must make the invisible informal systems in our workplaces as visible as possible. While many companies have formalized policies or processes for how information gets shared or promotions happen, there are informal systems that supersede these formalized procedures. You can tick every box in a formal policy and process to get promoted, but if you don't have the backing of the people who make the decision, it's unlikely to happen.

We like formal policies and processes because we believe this makes workplaces fairer. A 2018 article published in *Asia Pacific Management Review* states that some employees like formal policies and processes because having tangible standards for how people will be recruited, compensated, and promoted makes people believe the organization is fair. But no number of policies can guarantee that your coworkers will support your advancement. You can attend all the formal networking and leadership development events you like, but employees will only try to invest in building relationships with people they trust.

No matter how formal your workplace is, the four informal systems exist in every organization because these are the systems that build or break trust.

For example, does your organization include you? Do you have access to the information you need to do your job? Do you have opportunities to develop and advance? Do you believe your workplace has your best interests in mind? All these questions are examples of how informal systems relate to trust. When you don't know how to read the four informal systems, it's difficult for people to trust you because they cannot predict how you will behave. Even if I had managed every aspect of the ExCo meeting to perfection, my failure to build informal relationships with ExCo members would make it impossible for them to get to know me. The trust exchange depends on each of us knowing how to hold up our end of the bargain when it comes to building relationships, sharing information, and supporting one another's development and advancement. In other words, you know how to make your workplace work for you.

When Jo asked me to go to dinner, I thought I needed to go because it was the polite thing to do. Sure, getting to know the most senior leaders might help my career, but I felt obligated to go. What I missed in that interaction was the understanding that spending time with people in your organization is how you come to belong in your organization. When we get to know groups of people, like coworkers on a project, senior leadership teams, or your direct reports, we come to understand their common goals, behaviors, and values. Based on this understanding, you then decide whether you feel connected to your workplace—the extent to which you align with a company's leaders, employees, values, mission, and purpose—and want to work there. A 2014 study published in *Personnel Psychology* reviewed relevant literature on how people identify with their workplace. The study found you are more likely to build positive work relationships when there is a match between your character (including your goals, norms, behaviors, and values) and your workplace. When you identify with your workplace, you are more likely to be happier, perform better, and stay longer because you are more committed to the people in it. The more we identify with our workplace, the more we attach to it.

My research has found that when people work in the same group, like an ExCo, they create informal networks or social groups to collaborate effectively. Informal networks include any relationships you develop and maintain at work that are not formalized through an organizational hierarchy, like the formal relationship you have with your boss. Most organizations have formalized networking events, like peer groups, communities of practice, employee resource groups, committees, and ExCos, but what these formalized networks really do is bring people together so they can engage in informal networking to get to know one another and decide if and how they are going to work together.

Informal networks matter. The strength of your informal connections at work determines the support you are likely to get for a project, consensus on critical decisions, introductions to important people, and support for career advancement. The strength of your informal connections determines the strength of your informal network. The strength of our connections depends on our ability to build trust. Research has found that demonstrating sensitivity to people's needs and interests—reading the air—is critical to building trust because everyone wants to feel seen and heard. Taking the time to get to know your coworkers and what matters to them (like considering their unique viewpoints and aspirations) makes people feel seen, which builds trust.

Simply put: building informal networks is the key to succeeding at work. A 2008 study published in the *Academy of Management Journal* found that the most successful managers spend 70 percent more time engaged in networking activities and 10 percent more time communicating than their less successful counterparts.

Informal networks also significantly impact your ability to access valuable information and development and career opportunities. Research has found that about 70 percent of all jobs are not published or made publicly available, and consequently, 80 percent of vacant positions are filled through informal networks. Your ability to innovate, create, and get your next job depends on your ability to build an informal network.

Informal networks also give you access to the informal information you need to do your job. Informal information includes information shared casually, for instance, over virtual coffee or after-work drinks, to learn who supports a company decision or not and what team members get along. You might even gain insight into how your teammates perceive you. For anyone who has started a job with a new company during the pandemic, onboarding in a virtual work environment is challenging because there are almost no opportunities to access the informal information needed to understand how the organization works.

A 2013 research study published in the *Journal of Information and Knowledge Management* found that employees are much more likely to share valuable information when they trust their colleagues because they know it is safe to be themselves. The quality and range of social relationships you form at work determine the quality and range of informal information you have access to, like what organizational changes are happening, what promotional opportunities exist, why certain decisions are made, and who is supportive of them.

As you gain increased access to informal information through your workplace relationships, you build up your *organizational awareness*. Research finds that organizational awareness, which is understanding how your workplace works, is created by sharing informal information. And organizational awareness is the most crucial factor for responding to changes in your work environment because it includes how well you understand:

- Who do you need to work with, and how do you work with these people to get the job done?

- What informal workplace opportunities exist, and who can support you with accessing them?
- Who is willing to support your next career move and advocate on your behalf? How do you access career support if you don't have it?

We have to continually read the air because informal information constantly changes; organizational awareness is not fixed. When you are aware of and understand the informal side of working life, you have developed the organizational awareness you need to manage how you do your job. We build and maintain our organizational awareness through the informal information we access through our work relationships.

Not only do work relationships provide access to informal information, but they also determine your ability to develop new skills. Even when organizations have formalized processes for allocating work, my research has found that these companies still rely on informal recommendations when deciding who gets the top assignment. We like to work with people we already know because we trust them. To get people to support you, you need to show them that you are worthy of their support *because* you are someone they can trust. This is known in academia as the *norm of reciprocity*: "What we give is what we get."

Research has firmly established that when you believe your teammates value your contributions and care about your well-being, you will work harder and perform better in your job to pay back the support you have received. Likewise, when you feel like your team members don't support you, are out for themselves, or have betrayed your trust, you are more likely to slack off as a form of payback.

The norm of reciprocity is the unwritten rule for gaining the exposure you need to access development opportunities. When you show concern for your coworkers, openly share information, work hard, and include others, you are holding up your end of the bargain, and your teammates are more likely to trust you, which makes you feel supported and as if you belong. People will only support you if they trust you. When we support our teammate's career development by taking time to share advice, contacts, and opportunities, we build trust.

Trust is a two-way street. Yes, you need to be able to trust the people you work with, and for that, the organization has your best interests in mind, but *they* have to be able to trust that investing their time and energy in you is in *their* best interests.

To get ahead at work, you need to have people in your corner who are willing to advocate for your development and advancement—what I call *career advocates*. Very rarely are development or promotion decisions made on merit alone. You are not the sum of your achievements. Instead, your motivations, values, personality, and identity determine *how* you achieve outcomes, which is more important than *what* you achieve.

Getting promoted requires more than just high performance scores. Or a mentor (someone who provides you with advice and guidance). It isn't even enough to have a sponsor, who is often a person who might help you gain access to valuable connections and opportunities. To get promoted, you need a career advocate, someone with a vested interest in your success and who is willing to give you honest and direct feedback, promote your achievements, and make a case for your development and advancement.

Career advocates matter, as the 2011 study *The Sponsor Effect: Breaking Through the Last Glass Ceiling* by the Center for Work-Life Policy found. The study showed that people who advance have the backing of influential people who inspire and guide their careers. This backing makes it easier to ask for things like a promotion or a raise, as the study found most people without a career advocate resist confronting their manager about a raise. But when they have a career advocate, half of the respondents put themselves forward for a pay raise. So, to get that next promotion or pay increase, we need to understand who is in our corner and what these career advocates say about us when we're not in the room. Even more important, we need to know how to pay it forward and advocate for others.

Awareness and Engagement: How We Learn to Read the Air

When we read the air, we signal to our coworkers that we are trustworthy because our behavior lets people know we have their best interests in mind.

Learning to read the air includes two essential elements: awareness and engagement. First, you build your awareness and understanding of how workplaces work by getting to know the four informal systems: informal networks, informal information sharing, informal development, and informal advancement systems.

It isn't the formal aspects of your work environment—including official policies and processes—that will really impact your career success. If getting promoted were as easy as getting a degree, following a policy or process, or doing everything outlined in a job description to the letter, we would all be CEOs. But it's one thing to understand how your workplace *functions* and another to know how to make it *work for you*.

To build and maintain your informal networks, you must regularly engage in practices that build meaningful connections at work. Therefore, the second essential part of learning to read the air is engagement, which includes understanding how to navigate these four informal systems. In the following chapters, I will reveal how each of the four informal systems works and what behaviors—what I call *the practices*—you need to habitually engage in to manage how you build relationships, share information, and manage your development and career advancement. It isn't enough to know how your workplace works; it's what you do with this knowledge that counts.

Based on my research, everyone differs in their level of awareness and engagement. Our ability to read the air often coincides with our years of work experience because our awareness of the four informal systems (tacit knowledge) takes time to develop. Essentially, when it comes to reading the air, there are really four categories that most people fit into, as illustrated in Figure 1 below.

Learning To Read The Air

	Naïve	**Active**
High	*Individuals are aware of the four informal processes that exist in workplaces but choose not to read the air to navigate them.*	*Individuals are aware of the four informal processes that exist in workplaces and know how to read the air to navigate them*
	In Denial	**Active By Default**
Low	*Individuals are unaware of the four informal processes that exist in workplaces or deny them and choose not to read the air to navigate them.*	*Individuals are unaware of the four informal processes that exist in workplaces, but they know how to read the air to navigate them.*

Awareness (vertical axis)

Engagement — Low / High (horizontal axis)

Figure 1. Learning to Read the Air

For example, when you start your career, you may be *in denial* about the importance of managing the *how* of work. One of the reasons for this is that people like to believe workplaces are fair, transparent, and meritocratic. We want to know that people advance because of *what* they achieve. It is easier to trust companies when we have clarity, so we want to hold on to the notion that focusing on our tasks and fulfilling all the obligations in a job description means we are doing a good job.

But this all depends on your definition of a good job. Sure, in the past, simply fulfilling all the task requirements for positions below the managerial level might be enough to get by. But workplaces have changed dramatically in the last decade, especially following the pandemic. The hybridized organization is becoming increasingly ambiguous—for all the reasons I outlined in the introduction. We all have to manage the informal side of working life—regardless of where we sit in the organizational hierarchy. Denying this fact won't make it any less true. Doing a good job requires managing what we achieve and how we achieve it.

Three to five years into your career, it's likely that you have started to become aware of how the informal systems work in your organization and what you need to do to navigate them. But you might still not be convinced that this is something *you* must do to make it. At this point, some people choose not to engage in the practices that make up reading the air because they want to hold on to the belief that doing a good job is enough. After all, "reading the air" wasn't outlined in their job description when they took the job.

What they miss is the fact that doing a good job *is* reading the air—managing *the what* and *the how* is the new definition of success because how we work enables what we can achieve.

These individuals are often naïve about the negative impact that choosing not to read the air has on their careers.

From the manager level and up, most positions require the ability to manage the informal. One reason for this is that as you progress up an organizational ladder, you need to work with others to achieve anything. Learning to read the air and manage the informal side of working life becomes an essential skill. Once a person begins managing others, knowing how to read the air is essential because this skill determines their ability to work with people. They may not be able to tell you why they do what they do or how exactly the informal systems work, but they know how to navigate them almost intuitively. And they have learned this through trial and error, from observing people who succeed as well as those who fail, and from having more senior people share their knowledge and expertise as they relate to the job *as well as* the workplace.

It's normally around five to ten years into our careers that future leaders within the organization begin to emerge. What separates these rising stars from everyone else is they have learned to read the air. Consistently, people who are earmarked for future leadership positions read the air by learning how the informal systems work and engaging in the behaviors required to navigate them. There are very few exceptions to this rule in corporate positions. Certain technical positions, for example, may be exempted as they require a high degree of specialized skill and very little day-to-day interaction with others. But even these roles, as I shared in the introduction, will increasingly require some ability to read the air because they require the social and emotional skills to manage change, make complex decisions, and work with others to achieve outcomes. Meanwhile, jobs that involve a high degree of routine tasks, like proofreading, bookkeeping, or data entry, may not require the ability to read the air, but these types of jobs are likely to be replaced by automation at some point in the future, which is why learning how to read the air is something everyone can benefit from, regardless of their role.

At the end of the day, it doesn't really matter what kind of job you have—change will either happen to you, or you'll be the leader creating it.

What Reading the Air Gets You: Trust and Social Capital

Plenty of books and business magazine articles suggest that all you have to do to get ahead is make friends with people and influence them to support your advancement. After all, it's not what you know, it's who you know, so get out there and meet powerful people. But this advice assumes relationships are one-way, and it ignores that, much like a forest, workplaces are a community of individuals working together.

When we manage the how of work, we are building and maintaining our social capital. A 1997 study published in the journal *Economic Development and Cultural Change* found that social capital depends on individuals having frequent interaction, sharing helpful information, and following the norm of reciprocity by being willing to help one another. One informal system isn't more important than another; you need all four.

Researchers examining social capital find that your social capital can be measured by the degree of trust you have in your relationships with others. For example, in a work context, how much someone trusts you determines how willing they are to work with you, share their contacts, resources, and information, and advocate for your advancement. When you manage all four informal systems, you build the social capital you need to advance your career and connections at work.

Trust might link employees to their workplaces, but what's missing in the trust exchange is our awareness and understanding of how to build trust. In the following chapters, I will reveal how the four informal systems work and, importantly, what actions—what I call practices—you can take to build trust, navigate the informal, and manage the new normal of work.

3

INFORMAL NETWORKS

How to Gain Career-Defining Advice and Support

The Case for a New Networking Strategy

Throughout my career, whenever I started working for a new company, my boss or a coworker would, as part of the onboarding process, share the company organizational chart—a diagram that illustrates the structure of organizations, with positions, titles, ranks, and reporting lines. It only took a few minutes for someone to explain the formal structure. The real challenge was building my awareness of the informal relationships that exist outside of the formal structure. Who is connected to whom beyond formal titles? What team members like to work together? How strong are these relationships? Who can I trust?

While every company has a formal structure captured in an organizational chart, getting to know the informal network that lies beneath can be a lot harder. The informal networks that exist in workplaces are not mandated; rather, these relationships form organically. Employees excluded from a formal network (like when Rachel excluded me) can raise issues with their boss or human resources; however, not being invited to an informal gathering after work isn't something organizations typically manage.

Informal networks are the unofficial interpersonal relationships we have at work. Informal networks are not depicted in a formal organizational chart; instead, we form mental maps of our relationships, which are visual images or representations of the people we are connected to. In contrast, formal networks are relationships based on formalized contracts, reporting lines, hierarchies, and organizational structures. Formal networks tend to be officially established within the organization, their members are easily recognized, and the structure is explicit.

We are sold the idea that there is one type of network—a formal network—that we develop by attending after-work drinks or conferences and awkwardly introducing ourselves to random people so we can hand out a business card. This is the formal farce of working life because informal networking (the type of networking that has the most significant impact on your career) doesn't happen at formal events. Instead, informal networking occurs when we go for a coffee with a colleague or take a few minutes each morning to make small talk on Zoom with our teammates. These small acts, over time, help nurture the connections we need at work. Every informal connection you make becomes a part of your informal network, which includes people you can contact for information, advice, support, and the resources you need to do your job. *Your ability to do your job relies on the connections you cultivate.*

More than three decades of research has found that the informal connections you create at work help you find jobs, access opportunities for development and promotions, and increase your future earnings. Informal networks give you social capital in the form of advice, social support, and information. A 2016 research study stated that 30 percent of employees report having a close connection at work. Close relationships provide employees with support, advice, and access to information, increasing productivity, retention, and job satisfaction. Employees with close relationships at work are seven times more likely to be engaged in their work than employees who do not have these types of relationships. Some people provide guidance, others provide mental and emotional support, and others share their knowledge, expertise, and insights.

In 2020, my first book, *The Fix*, came out, and in the first year, I spoke about the book at many events—482 to be exact. Most events were virtual. At every event, people had an opportunity to ask questions. The first question I always got asked was: Why is it so hard to hire diverse talent? To which I explained that informal networks are often how we access jobs. As I shared in chapter two, nearly 70 percent of all jobs are not published or made publicly available, and consequently, 80 percent of vacant positions are filled through informal networks. When you have a vacancy on your team, who might you approach to apply for the role? If you are a hiring manager struggling to hire diverse talent into your organization, it could be a sign that your informal networks are not diverse.

In the past, having a "closed" informal network—an informal network where members are pretty similar to one another and do not develop relationships with people who are different—didn't matter. Typically, white men have and still do dominate leadership positions in organizations, and most research has found their networks are closed. The term "old boys' club" describes the phenomenon whereby white men typically build informal relationships with people who are similar to them, to the exclusion of everyone else.

When white men have closed informal networks, they tend to offer helpful information, opportunities for development, and the endorsement needed to secure promotion exclusively to members within that network because these are the people they know and trust. It's not uncommon to like people who are more like you because they tend to be easier to read. It's easy to predict how people who are similar to us will behave or what they value, making it easier to trust them. The cost to organizations, however, is not only a lack of equity and diversity but groupthink, as people with the same backgrounds and perspectives tend to approach work the same way, limiting innovation, creativity, and the ability to solve complex problems.

While it might be tempting to assume the old boys' club is a thing of the past, it isn't. A study published in a 2021 *Harvard Business Review* article titled "Research: We're Losing Touch with Our Networks" found that in large part, thanks to hybrid working, the diversity of individual networks shrank by close to 16 percent, as people were more likely to connect with existing close contacts (like the people they sit with at lunch) than with people they don't know. This drop-off is explained mainly by men, whose networks shrank by 30 percent, while women's networks only reduced a little. While having a closed network might have worked in the past, the world of work has changed.

Not diversifying your network isn't an option.

Your ability to do your job requires building and maintaining a wide range of contacts. For example, a 2011 research study published in a *Harvard Business Review* article titled "A Smarter Way to Network" found that executives who consistently rank in the top 20 percent of their companies (both in terms of performance and employee well-being) have diverse networks, made up of people who come from a range of backgrounds, positions, and levels within the organization. Additionally, a 2012 research study published in *MIT Sloan Management Review* titled *Cultivating an Inclusive Culture Through Personal Networks* found that people with more diverse networks were not only more likely to be promoted and remain with their organization for a longer period, but the diversity of their network enabled them to solve problems more innovatively and creatively. We need mentoring, sponsorship, advice, and career coaching from a diverse range of people at work because this is how we obtain a greater variety of support required to manage all the challenges we face on the other side.

While the old boys' network might have worked in the past, it's no longer an effective career development strategy. As any hiring manager struggling to recruit talent from typically underrepresented groups knows, most leaders only network with people who look like them.

The motivation to build a diverse informal network is simple: we need them. Without a diverse network, it won't be easy to survive. The constant changes brought on by technological advancements, globalization, shifting organizational structures, and the diversification of talent and customers require the ability to learn new skills. Careers today are boundaryless, as new jobs are constantly emerging. Research has found most employees will change their jobs on average every four and a half years. In an ever-changing work environment, you need to be flexible, mobile, and willing to learn new skills to stay relevant and valuable to your employer.

Consequently, your workplace is no longer responsible for managing your career path—you are. To survive, you must continually update and remarket your skills to meet the changes in your work environment. In the new world of work, having a diverse range of individuals advocating for your career will allow you to take advantage of the diverse range of career opportunities on offer. A 2013 research study by Ron Burt, a globally recognized network scientist, found that according to multiple peer-reviewed studies, simply being in an open network rather than a closed one is the best predictor of career success. Relying on the old boys' network to get your next promotion or job opportunity simply won't cut it.

Read the Air:
The Three Informal Networks You Need

I always assumed I wasn't very good at networking because I am introverted and like being alone more than being with others. But a 2002 *MIT Sloan Management Review* study found that personality isn't as crucial to networking as you might think. The study found that people with high-quality informal networks are not extroverted or introverted; they do things differently. For starters, they don't just focus on competing tasks at work; instead, they "read the air" by considering how to get the job done by intentionally and systematically building their informal networks. This includes taking stock of which relationships could be strengthened by spending time catching up with different people in an informal network or growing their network by getting to know new people. These individuals always seem to have lists of people they are trying to meet or planning to connect with.

Additionally, a 2008 study published in *Organizational Dynamics* examined the networks of high-performing employees in the top 20 percent of the organization's performance ratings. The study revealed high performers understand their networks and their role within their networks at work; they spend time developing connections that can extend their expertise and help advance their careers. When we don't know what informal connections we have, we don't understand what existing relationships need our attention or where we need to spend time developing new relationships.

Knowing who you turn to for what is the starting point for understanding how your networks work. Researchers have identified many types of informal networks, like social networks, like people you mix with at work, or knowledge networks, like the people with whom you share different insights. But when it comes to managing the how of work, my research has found there are three types of networks, including advice, social support, and information networks, that provide employees with the social capital they need to excel at work.

Informal Advice Networks

Even though we have more access to information than ever before in human history, a 2002 research study published in *MIT Sloan Management Review* found that even engineers and scientists were five times more likely to turn to friends or colleagues for information than to impersonal sources like Google.

Your informal advice network includes the people you go to for advice regarding a challenge or problem you are experiencing at work, like how to gain support for an idea or approval for promotion, etc. The advice you receive doesn't happen in a structured way through performance reviews; instead, it occurs casually through unscheduled talks, impromptu Slack chats, or Zoom calls. It's far easier to ask a close colleague for guidance at work than to ask your boss because you don't have to worry that you will be judged as a poor performer.

When you first join a company, developing an advice network is critical to understanding how to do your job because the guidance you receive from this informal network is the tacit knowledge you need to get things done. For example, think about when you started a job and the people who helped you understand the company jargon, how to pitch an idea or gain support for a critical decision. Then write down all the people you might seek out for similar guidance at work.

Combined, the names on the lists are your informal advice network.

Informal Social Support Networks

Your informal social support network is the people you turn to for encouragement, support, or help with professional or personal challenges. This includes people you feel comfortable sharing your feelings with and who will be there for you during the good times, like when you get a promotion, and the bad, such as when your job is at risk of redundancy.

Research has found that while advice networks increase our tacit knowledge through the guidance we receive, social support networks increase our tacit knowledge *and* performance. This is because social support networks provide essential emotional support (like coping with the isolation associated with remote work) and development advice (like learning to manage a demanding boss). Cultivating an informal social support network matters because these individuals provide the advice you need to manage challenges that can hinder or enhance your career development.

Importantly, informal social support networks are made up of people you trust to share a delicate work- or personal-related matter. They are tight-lipped and fair, usually avoiding gossip, and are not threatened by others' successes. These people are less interested in juicy details and more focused on brainstorming solutions.

When building an informal social support network, it's important to include people who you believe are both trustworthy (as you can count on them to keep your confidence and best interests front of mind) and knowledgeable enough to offer advice on a work-related challenge.

Informal Informational Networks

When we work with others, research has found, we build mental models (images in our minds) of our coworkers regarding who has what expertise, skills, preferences, and weaknesses. For teams to function effectively, everyone needs to know what they can contribute, who to go to for what, and how to work together. These mental models represent our informal information networks. Often referred to as the grapevine or watercooler chat, informal informational networks include the people you go to who can provide information on *how the informal workplace works*. Examples of the knowledge these networks provide include understanding who has relationships with whom, what changes might be happening in the broader organization, how these changes might potentially impact you, and who you can go to for support with a task or project. Informal information networks enable teamwork and a sense of belonging at work.

Informal informational networks are built up over time as we come to understand who to go to for what. The mental models represent our understanding of who's who at work and what relationships our coworkers have. We need this information to understand how to work with our teammates, as most of what we achieve at work happens through collaboration with other people. Information is communicated through the grapevine faster, as people know who to reach out to, and it's accurate 75–90 percent of the time. However, research has found that supervisors without informal information networks are 50 percent less likely to access credible information than those with these networks, negatively impacting their performance.

As your work environment changes with downsizing, hybrid working, and role changes due to technological advancements, your relationships at work will change. No informal networks are static. They take time and effort to manage because they are constantly changing. Every informal network offers different types of social capital—information, social support, or advice—needed to perform and advance at work. To build informal networks, you need to be aware of the three types of networks and then engage in the practices that will help you develop and maintain these connections.

Map Your Network: The Five Practices

In 1932, psychiatrist Dr. Jacob Levy Moreno researched why, in just two short weeks, a significant number of fourteen-year-old girls ran away from the Hudson School for Girls. According to a 2014 article published in *Slate* by Dr. Moreno's son, Jonathan Moreno, instead of investigating each case separately, Dr. Moreno mapped all fourteen girls in a visual diagram to illustrate how each girl influenced another to run away. By showing these informal connections, Dr. Moreno demonstrated the relationship between individual connections and group outcomes, which ultimately helped the school tackle its runaway epidemic. The technical name for Dr. Moreno's map is a *sociogram*, a graphic illustration of a person's relationships. Dr. Moreno's work has greatly influenced the understanding of personal and social networks. Social networking sites like Facebook are essentially based on the idea of a sociogram. But unlike Facebook, a sociogram doesn't only reflect the connections people share; it indicates the strength of the relationship and the nature of the association—that is, how close or loose a tie is.

When you map your networks, you build a map of who you trust, which also tells you who you don't. For example, the fourteen-year-old girls who decided to run away trusted one another, and based on the strength of their relationship and the connections they shared with other girls, Dr. Moreno could predict who would run away next.

Mapping your network is vital because this is how you become aware of your connections. This is how you learn to read your network by seeing who you are connected to and how diverse, beneficial, and close your contacts are. And with this awareness you can begin to take action and build relationships you might be lacking—and see why you don't have the information, support, and advice you need to succeed. Anyone can read, build, and maintain their informal networks by mapping them, which includes five read-the-air practices.

Practice 1: Make It Visible

Whether or not we are aware of it, every one of us has a unique mental image of the relationships in our workplace, but some people's mental maps are more accurate than others'. Informal network accuracy is the ability to correctly determine the type of connections *we* share with our colleagues (i.e., advice, social support, and information connections). But informal network accuracy also includes our ability to correctly determine the type, strength, and nature of *our colleagues'* informal connections. When you have a solid understanding of which coworkers you can trust at work, you know which of your teammates will work together, cooperate, and support one another. You can read the air because you know who to trust.

When you read relationships, you can predict how your colleagues are likely to engage with each other, making it easier to know how they are likely to behave and, therefore, how to engage and collaborate with them. This helps you avoid pitfalls, gain support for an idea or promotion, access important information, and influence decision-making. Knowing your informal network makes it easier for you to do your job.

To map your network, first decide which of the three networks you want to evaluate—your advice, social support, or informational network. Then, on a lined piece of paper, draw five columns. In the first column, write down the names of all the people within that particular informal network. For example, if you want to diagnose your informal advice network, then write down all the names of people you trust to guide you with a problematic issue, feedback, or career advancement. This list is your informal network.

Review each name on the list to decide if the person is more similar or more different from you in terms of your demographic characteristics, i.e., gender orientation, race, age, ethnicity, social class, sexual orientation, etc. Then in the second column, write down your response—*more similar* or *more different*—next to each name.

To map your network, it is important to understand who you are connected to and how strong and beneficial the relationship is. Later in this chapter, I share why investing in building mutually beneficial relationships is important.

To review how strong your connections are, take a look at each name on the list and decide if the relationship with each person is mutually beneficial as both parties benefit from the connection or one-way as only one person benefits from the relationship. Then, in the third column, write down your response—*mutually beneficial* or *one-way*—next to each name.

In this chapter, I will also share why it is important to have a mix of close relationships and loose acquaintances in an informal network. To determine the strength of a relationship, review each name on the list and decide if it is a close or loose connection. A close connection includes a relationship with someone you trust, whereas a loose connection includes relationships with people you don't know well enough to predict how they will behave. To review how close or loose your connections are, look at each name on the list and decide if you know the person well enough to trust them and can predict how they will behave. Then, in the fourth column, write down your response—*close* or *loose*—next to each name.

Now that you have made a map of your informal network, you can navigate it by putting the remaining practices into action.

Practice 2: Diversify Your Network

I have been coaching Chris, a CEO of a multimillion-dollar mobile personal training business, for two years. Chris started his career in the fitness industry as a personal trainer working twelve-hour shifts in a local gym. Within a year, Chris had over 120 clients and enough money to venture out on his own and build his first mobile gym business. Chris puts all his success down to one thing: he can build a relationship with just about anyone.

I call Chris a superconnector, as he knows how to build relationships and work with hundreds of people from all walks of life. It is unusual to be a superconnector. Establishing and maintaining relationships requires time, attention, and energy, which can be exhausting. According to a 2017 study published in *Harvard Business Review*, the ideal number of connections in an informal network at work is anywhere from twelve to eighteen people. If your network consists of fewer connections than this, think about which people you might want to introduce yourself to or take out for a cup of coffee to build your informal network. If your informal network consists of more contacts than eighteen, it can be challenging to manage. This is especially true if you devote time to developing all three informal networks and have different people in each of these networks. You can't connect to everyone. There isn't an unlimited amount of you to go around, so you must be strategic about where you invest your time and energy.

Superconnectors typically have extensive, diverse networks. They build and maintain their networks by engaging in specific behaviors—like diversifying their networks. Even at school, Chris made it a habit to get to know kids who were often left out (like me) or didn't share his white, middle-class, heterosexual, able-bodied identity.

I asked Chris what motivates him to connect across differences; he looked at me with a confused expression and replied, "It makes life so much more interesting. Who wants to hang out with the same people every day?"

Review your list again. How often do the words *more similar* appear in column two? For example, do people on your list share your demographic characteristics, background, expertise, organizational level, and function? Based on my research, you have a diverse network if at least half of the connections you form include people with different demographic characteristics from you.

Most of the time, we limit our connections to people who are similar to us. That's why a 2005 research study published in *Harvard Business Review* revealed that if you build your network by introducing yourself to people more than 65 percent of the time, you are probably building a network that includes people who are relatively similar to you. The more diverse a network is in terms of the demographic characteristics of the people within your networks, the more varied the range of information, advice, and social support it offers.

To diversify your network, you need to think about how you are growing your network. When Chris meets a client for the first time, he makes sure to share who he is. He talks about his family and where he grew up and went to school. He makes it safe for people to share who they are by revealing who he is. Then he gets to know the other person by asking questions. Lots of questions.

Chris says, "It's all about finding the points of connection—what makes someone who they are, what they care about, and what makes them tick."

Most relationships are built on similarity because getting to know people who share your hobbies or interests is easy. But superconnectors bridge their differences with others by finding the points of connection, which include the things other people care about. Once they find these connection points, they demonstrate an interest in learning more about that topic. For example, when Chris was in school, he was the only white kid who made an effort to get to know a group of Japanese exchange students in his year. He did this by taking an interest in their passion for anime, a computer-generated animation originating in Japan, and being curious about it. Chris takes the practice of building points of connection so seriously that he will research a client before meeting them to understand what they might be interested in and then ask them questions about this topic when they meet. This is how superconnectors invest in their informal networks.

Diversifying your network isn't simply a case of handing your business card to people who don't look like you. Instead, it is about devoting time and attention—like Chris—to getting to know different people.

Practice 3: Invest in Mutually Beneficial Relationships

One of the common mistakes people make in building relationships at work is assuming that just because they know someone well, the connection is worth investing in. Relationships change and develop over time. A 2013 study published in *Administrative Science Quarterly* found that connections stand the test of time when people reflect on the quality of their relationships and manage their shared experiences. The strength of a connection reflects how well both people know one another, but the connection's quality reflects how healthy and well functioning the relationship is. Mutually beneficial relationships are the connections you share that have a high degree of trust, reciprocity, and active engagement from both individuals. The quality of your relationship is determined by how mutually beneficial it is.

The more connected you are to people in your work environment, the more self-confidence, social support, advice, and meaning you will experience. We need mutually beneficial relationships, as research has found they improve work performance, learning, development, and sense of belonging. They also enable feelings of psychological safety, trust, and well-being. Quality relationships increase our ability to deal with stress; some studies have even found they increase our immunity and lower our blood pressure, increasing our life span. Mutually beneficial relationships are literally life-affirming.

By contrast, one-way connections include relationships that deplete us. These connections have low trust, reciprocity, and engagement from both individuals. Often one-way relationships include the people we must work with but wouldn't choose to spend time with or where we are unsure if a person has our best interests in mind. Even a tiny number of one-way connections can harm your psychological well-being. According to a 2011 study published in *Harvard Business Review,* roughly 90 percent of anxiety at work is created by 5 percent of the people in your informal network.

But being aware of your negative connections helps to counteract these effects. A key reason for this is ambiguous relationships—where you are unsure if someone has your best interests in mind—are draining. When you don't know if someone likes you, trusts you, or is willing to support you, you are not sure if you should invest time building the relationship. Consequently, you spend a lot of mental energy deciding what to do, which can be exhausting.

To overcome these challenges, you need to know what type of relationships you have. A 2017 academic journal article published in *Group and Organization Management* found that simply being aware of your negative connections counteracts the negative psychological impact of these connections. Simply "knowing thy enemy" allows you to manage any challenges you associate with this relationship or avoid the person.

Identifying mutually beneficial relationships that provide you with the most support is helpful—known as high-quality connections. A 2003 study published in *Positive Organizational Scholarship: Foundations of a New Discipline* found that high-quality relationships have three essential attributes. These include both parties sharing positive and negative emotions, being able to disagree and maintain the relationship, and being open to new ideas and different ways of doing things. Even if you move to a new organization or country, you are more likely to maintain a relationship if it has these three features.

To examine the quality of your relationships, review the names on your list for the ones you identified as mutually beneficial (in column three) and ask yourself the following questions:

- Do you feel safe sharing feelings, challenges, and problems you are encountering with the other person?
- Do you discuss disagreements? Can you remain friends, even if you hold different beliefs, opinions, and perspectives?
- Do you feel comfortable sharing your ambitions, aspirations, and ideas with the other person?

If you answered yes to each of these questions, then it is highly likely that your relationship is a high-quality connection, which means you need to do the work to keep it.

To build mutually beneficial relationships, you need to create a pool of goodwill, which means being willing to help people even if they have not asked for it. A 2012 research study published in *MIT Sloan Management Review* found (regardless of a person's gender or racial ethnicity) that employees who were promoted quickly and stayed with their companies for a long time had one thing in common—they reached out to key stakeholders to understand their needs and used their capabilities to try to meet those needs. By reaching out and trying to be helpful, these employees demonstrated the norm of reciprocity, and in doing so, they became more visible to important people. In addition, they showed their value by offering their expertise, ideas, and social support. As a result, they had built reputations for reliability, which is the basis of trust. They also followed the rule of reciprocity that governs the trust exchange by creating the belief that they cared about their colleagues and had their interests in mind.

Creating goodwill is about recognizing that when you behave with other people's best interests at heart, you signal to individuals that you are trustworthy. For example, when you offer informal information, social support, or advice to someone who hasn't asked for it, you strengthen your connection because you demonstrate that you trust them. Consistently, research has found when we engage in these types of reciprocal supportive exchanges at work, it increases productivity, promotes learning, and builds a culture of trust. You trust that the relationship is mutually beneficial, which strengthens the connection you share. Doing this with enough people in your network increases the general perception of your trustworthiness. When you create a pool of goodwill, you become someone in your network who is worth knowing.

Practice 4: Invest in a Mix of Connections

While demographic diversity matters, research has also found that the quality of your networks substantially impacts your ability to solve problems, undertake projects, and execute a plan at work. Your connection with someone in your advice, social support, or information network is referred to by researchers as a tie. How strong or close a relationship is—the tie—reflects how much you trust someone. Close ties include people you interact with frequently and feel comfortable sharing your ideas or concerns with or asking for help and advice. Loose ties include any relationships that have infrequent interaction and minimal emotional closeness. For example, your loose ties might include coworkers you chat with at the work cafeteria or on Slack. Loose ties provide you with insight into how your workplace functions, as well as access to novel information.

Close ties are typically associated with increased performance because they are more likely to provide you with the tacit knowledge, career advice, and support needed to do your job well. Close ties also matter when it comes to job and career satisfaction. For example, a 2016 study published in *Work and Occupations* found that the social support that close ties provide improves employees' mental and emotional well-being more than career opportunities.

Just because close ties play an essential role in career advancement doesn't mean that loose ties are bad. Close ties tend to include people who are close to you and probably share similar contacts. However, loose ties are the acquaintances you know who can connect you to others in an informal network. When you have loose ties with diverse networks, they will likely have connections you don't have but might need. Research has found that loose ties are more helpful than close contacts for finding a job because they connect you to other informal networks and people you might not otherwise know. Close ties, however, will give you the advice and support needed to secure the job. A high-quality network has a combination of close and loose ties.

Take another moment to consider your informal network by reviewing each name in column four—close or loose connection—on your list. While there is no perfect number of close versus loose ties, you should have more loose ties than close ties. That's because close connections take a lot of time and energy to manage. A 2018 study published in *Human Resource Management* found that you need at least one close tie to provide access to informal information, which, in turn, will help you understand organizational changes and decisions and identify career opportunities. In addition, you need at least one person in your informal networks who can provide support if you are having a bad day. This is someone who helps you manage your mental and emotional well-being and work-life balance. In addition, you need at least two close ties that will give you career advice and support your advancement at work. This includes people who can provide developmental feedback, challenge your decisions, and encourage you to do better.

If you don't have some or any of these types of relationships, then it's time to devote yourself to building them. Investing in mutually beneficial relationships is how you develop close connections, whereas loose connections are formed by creating opportunities to connect. In the interviews I conducted for my PhD participants revealed how instrumental shared experiences are to creating and keeping informal networks. When I started researching the topic, I thought shared experiences only included attending Friday drinks or playing golf—old boys' club activities. But I soon discovered people build relationships through shared experiences at work, like working on a task with a colleague or making a pitch to a client. When employees work on something together, they bond over the experience. Opportunities to work on a project, special initiative, or a team-building activity all facilitate the development of trust because people learn to work together toward a common goal, and in doing so, they get to know one another—this is exposure.

In building loose connections, the more a person has exposure to you, the easier it is for them to collaborate with you because they know who you are. This is the trust exchange. If you want to grow the number of people in your informal network, you'll need to identify what proportion of your day is spent working alone and what opportunities you may have to enroll others in the delivery of your work. Even if you cannot directly work with someone on a project, you can still share what you are working on and seek out others' input, advice, ideas, or opinions on how to go about it.

Practice 5: Diversify Your Role

Whether you know it or not, you perform a role within your network. Knowing the role you perform helps you understand how other people within your informal network perceive you. Our positions in a network often reflect different aspects of who we are. For example, take a moment to think about whether people in your organization come to you for work-related advice. If they do, this is a sign that you are perceived as trustworthy, competent, and influential. If most people come to you for information, then it might be a sign you are seen as someone who has access to helpful information because of the number of connections you have.

Based on decades of research, academics have identified various roles people perform in networks. Based on my research, I have condensed these roles into four types: connectors, bridges, brokers, and experts.

Connectors tend to be people at the center of any network as they link people within the network. These people tend to be very influential as they are associated with most people within the network, who seek them out for support and advice. Connectors tend to have a lot of close ties within a network, and they are sought out for help, advice, and information, making them highly influential.

A *bridge* is someone at work who knows people in two different groups and then connects some people in each group or in both groups. Unlike connectors, bridges only have close connections with some people within an informal network, but they have many loose connections in multiple informal networks. Often bridges are sought out for *who they know* and for advice on who to go to for what. Generally, bridges include people who find it easy to make connections and are socially confident.

A *broker* is someone who shares information within their informal networks. Often this is someone who always seems to be the first to know what is going on and is willing to share what they know. Brokers may only have a few close and loose ties within a network but are a part of numerous diverse networks. The diversity of connections that brokers have provides them with access to a wide range of novel or unique information. These people are typically sought out for advice on *how to get things* done because they know a diverse range of people who can help with just about any task. Brokers usually include people who find it easy to connect across differences and enjoy meeting people from diverse backgrounds.

The expert has only a few close and loose connections within a network, but their connections rely on them for critical skills or knowledge. Experts not only limit the bonds they form within a network but are typically only connected to a few informal networks. These individuals are regularly sought out for *what they know*. Experts are the people who have the experience, skills, insights, and ability to help solve complex problems at work. Informal networks rely on experts to provide critical advice on a problematic work-related issue or complex task.

While you can perform multiple roles in an informal network, you tend to occupy one role more than the others. Your role may change over time as your relationships or informal networks change. The role you tend to occupy the most reflects how most people perceive you within the informal network. You can also use the role descriptions outlined in this chapter to understand the various roles that other people perform in an informal network. When you can read the different roles people occupy in an informal network, you understand the unique value everyone brings to the trust exchange, making it easier to collaborate.

For example, I know that I tend to occupy the role of an expert in my informal networks, and someone who is a connector might find it challenging to get to know me initially. But if they understood the role of an expert in a network, they would understand the value I have to offer. When I meet a connector like Chris, I often feel overwhelmed by their outgoing nature, but I value these relationships tremendously because they keep me connected to the informal network.

To manage your position within your network, first, review the descriptors for each role within an informal network and decide which one you occupy most. Second, take time to understand other people's roles by examining the four positions in a network and deciding which one they most often fill. If there is someone you want to connect with or someone you are struggling to connect with, consider whether you understand the role they occupy and how to connect with them. Third, consider if you can strengthen your connection by finding different ways to collaborate with them. For example, you can establish a relationship with connectors by offering information, social support, and advice. For bridges and brokers, you can connect by sharing your contacts and making introductions. Finally, for experts, you can offer exciting information or share your expertise.

The 2019 study *Social Capital and Career Growth*, published in the *International Journal of Manpower*, found that we build our social capital through deliberate goal-oriented investments in various relationships. This means being aware that different relationships provide different types of support. When you distrust someone, you often misunderstand the role they fulfill or expect them to behave the same as you. When they don't, you devalue their differences, which makes it easy to exclude them from the social support, advice, and information you might share with others. When we understand the roles people fulfill in informal networks, we understand how they differ from us, which makes it easier to value the unique contribution each has to offer.

Make Trust a Habit

If you Google *baseball* and *unwritten rules*, you will find hundreds of references to the unofficial practices players must adhere to when playing the game. While there are formalized rules in baseball, numerous informal practices reinforce etiquette and sportsmanship. Getting to know the informal practices is something players do over time by watching other players, making mistakes, and listening to others share what they know. These rules matter precisely because teammates are less likely to trust them if a player breaks them.

In 2020, an article in the *Guardian* shared how Fernando Tatís Jr., a professional baseball player for the San Diego Padres, was criticized for driving too many runs. While this may seem strange in a game where driving up runs is how a team wins, the expectation—the informal practice—is that when one team (Team A) is the front-runner, and the other team (Team B) is expected to lose, Team A won't run up the score; gaining runs for the sake of gaining runs is considered unsportsmanlike. This is such a well-established rule that Tatís should have known better, which is why the *Guardian* published a story on it. And just to be sure Tatís adhered to the rule, the *Guardian* reported that Tatís's manager, Jayce Tingler, gave him a sign that indicated he should not swing at the 3–0 pitch. But unfortunately, Tatís failed to read the air.

When we fail to read the air, it makes us less trustworthy. Like Tatís, we can bring down the reputation of the whole team. Once our teammates cannot predict how we will behave, they are less likely to support us and our goals.

Safe to say, it's challenging to do your job when you do not trust the people you work with. Engaging in the five practices to create and maintain your informal networks is how you signal to your teammates that you are trustworthy.

4

INFORMAL INFORMATION

How to Be in the Know

Earlier, I shared the story of a Japanese businessman who failed to read the air because he lacked self-awareness. The Japanese businessman had to know what his client needed to prevent the meeting from ending badly. As an extremely busy leader overseeing a Fortune 500 company, time mattered most to his client. Had the Japanese businessperson paid attention, he would have noticed his client kept looking at his watch and moving in his chair because he needed the meeting to end.

Most of us remember moments when we tuned out and failed to read the air. We learn how to behave in different situations by seeking informal feedback or picking up on hints or cues from social interactions. We use this information to guide and adjust our behavior to align with the needs and expectations of the people we engage with.

As I outlined in chapter two, our ability to read the air requires awareness of our informal work environment and engagement in the practices outlined in this book to navigate it. Our awareness is made up of how well we understand ourselves, other people, and our work environment.

The Japanese businessman was not aware of how he was being perceived. He also didn't understand his client's needs because he wasn't reading the informal cues correctly. In any organization, there are two types of information, formal and informal. Formal information includes information that is clearly and explicitly communicated in things like company policies, processes, handbooks, newsletters, annual reports, or company statements. On the other hand, informal information generally includes information about your workplace that is difficult to articulate formally—like sensing when a meeting is coming to an end. Our ability to access informal information determines how well we can read the air—like knowing what matters most to a client. Accessing informal information helps us understand ourselves, other people, and our workplace—it's the key that unlocks our ability to read the air.

Self-Awareness

I have worked in human resources for almost two decades, and during this time, I have helped managers provide underperforming employees with developmental feedback. Often managers ask me if a poor-performing employee will make it. And I always say the same thing. "That depends. Are they surprised by the feedback?"

In my experience, when employees are surprised by performance feedback, it often indicates that they lack awareness of their strengths and weaknesses or other people's perceptions of their capability. The more surprised someone is, the less awareness they often have. So the difficulty isn't simply improving performance. Instead, you need to know how a person views their performance and how others view their performance, and then identify gaps between these perceptions and agree on what needs to be developed.

Self-awareness is the difference between how we see ourselves and how others see us. Self-awareness requires three essential ingredients.

First, you have to know who you are, which means being aware of your thoughts, feelings, and behaviors because this information helps you understand why you do what you do. Second, you need to know if how you see yourself (in terms of your thoughts, feelings, and behaviors) matches how other people see you. Third, you need to know how to adjust your thoughts, feelings, and behaviors to resolve any mismatch between how you see yourself and how others see you.

In most cases, by the time a person has a formal performance conversation, it is too late. They are in the meeting because they failed to understand how others perceive them—to read the air. How others perceive you is often communicated informally, like an in-the-moment comment about your behavior on a project or a casual conversation with a colleague who suggests trying a different approach in a meeting.

We can also build our self-awareness by seeking out informal information to understand how others perceive us. The informal information we receive from coworkers, like friendly advice, feedback, suggestions, or guidance, serves as a mirror to tell us how our colleagues are experiencing us. When people are self-aware, they understand the gap between how they see themselves in terms of performance or behavior and how others see them. They don't simply rely on their own assessment but calibrate how they see themselves by including other people's perspectives in their overall assessment. As a result, self-aware people are also able to identify what they need to do to close the gap between how other people see them and how they see themselves.

When an employee is fired for poor performance, often it's because they don't understand the impact of their behavior on others or how to close the gap by changing their behavior. When a person is self-aware, they are mindful of their thoughts, feelings, and behaviors and the impression they have on other people. As a result, they actively manage how they come across to ensure they positively contribute to their work environment.

Other Awareness

Self-awareness alone isn't enough to read the air. The more we understand our thoughts, feelings, and behaviors, the easier it is to understand other people. Empathy is the ability to recognize how another person may feel and understand why they think or behave in a particular way. You can empathize with others only to the extent you can empathize with yourself. You can't know what it is like to walk in someone else's shoes unless you can walk in your own. Self-awareness enables other awareness. And other awareness enables self-awareness.

Our growth and development happen through the relationships we develop at work because these relationships provide us with an understanding of what we need to do to improve. Other awareness includes understanding another person's thoughts, feelings, and behavior—e.g., when a person knows that a client looking at their watch indicates that they need the meeting to end. To read the air, we need to become other aware, which requires that we know and understand the people we work with—i.e., why do our colleagues think, behave, and feel the way they do? Other awareness is the ability to distinguish between your behavior, thoughts, and emotions and other people's. It also includes knowing how your behavior impacts other people's behavior, thoughts, and emotions. Meaning that you understand what your clients need and how stressed they might feel if the meeting runs over, and they are late for their next appointment.

When we understand the people we work with, we feel connected to them and want to maintain this connection by investing in the relationship. This is because when we understand how other people think, feel, and behave and we believe they understand us in the same way, we feel seen, heard, and valued for who we are. Being connected to our coworkers makes us feel like we belong. Indeed, a 2012 academic research study published in *The Oxford Handbook of Positive Organizational Scholarship* found that when an individual has a high degree of other awareness, it increases their commitment, satisfaction, and sense of belonging at work.

Other awareness isn't a onetime effort to get to know your coworkers. It is a practice. It requires curiosity about other people's feelings, needs, motivations, and concerns. This means asking questions, listening, learning, and understanding another person's perspective. When you know the people you work with, you can correctly interpret and explain their thoughts, feelings, and behavior. When you know what people do and why they do it, this informal information provides insight into your behaviors. It helps you understand why you do what you do. The more you know someone, the more you can make accurate predictions about how they may think, feel, and behave in response to your behavior and different situations.

I deliver hundreds of workshops to clients worldwide to develop their organizational cultures. My clients often invite me to drinks and dinner to connect when I finish facilitating a workshop. But what I need is to go to my hotel and not talk to anyone for at least twelve hours. I am an introvert, and carving out alone time is critical to my well-being because it's how I recharge. If you know yourself, then you know what you need to be effective. If you know the people you work with, then you know what they need to be effective. As I have spent time getting to know my clients, I know which ones are extroverted and introverted. So I can predict who will likely want to go for dinner after a workshop. To manage their needs (and my own), I try to find a compromise by suggesting we meet for breakfast or lunch (and I try to do this before they invite me to dinner!). The most influential people in organizations know who they are working with, pay attention to how other people react, and try to respond in a way that meets other people's needs as well as their own.

Organizational Awareness

When we have to collaborate virtually or in a hybrid way, performance often suffers because, as research has confirmed, establishing trust remotely between teammates can be difficult. It is too easy to hold a biased view of a situation or make snap judgments of a person. For example, if you are in a Zoom meeting and a person's camera is off, it's easy to assume they are not paying attention or doing something else. Snap judgments are more prolific in virtual environments, where we see people for a short period and use this small interaction to decide who a person is. In a virtual setting, you recall uncommon behavior (like a person having their camera off) more likely than typical behavior (all the times that day they have shown up with it on). We give more weight to uncommon experiences when forming judgments about other people, like thinking our colleague is disengaged for having their camera off. Judgments are sticky; once we make them, they can be hard to shift because we look for evidence to confirm what we believe is true.

We make biased assessments of people and situations, especially in a virtual setting, because we don't understand another person's context and how they perceive the situation. For example, if a colleague isn't feeling well, they might dial in to the Zoom call with the camera off to demonstrate how committed they are! In an in-person meeting, you can sit face-to-face and see that your colleague doesn't look well, which demystifies what's happening. Research finds that when distant employees have made time to get to know one another, they work better together. These employees understand one another and know the other people's work environments and specific challenges or constraints. They also understand how their coworkers perceive them. They are, therefore, better placed to offer advice or share resources and expertise.

You develop other awareness when you learn how your coworkers like to work, who they have relationships with, and what their work environment is like. But when you know how your coworkers perceive how you like to work, your relationships, and your work environment, you have developed organizational awareness—because you understand how your workplace perceives you.

Mary, a CEO I regularly coach, had difficulty getting along with her chief financial officer (CFO) but didn't know why the relationship wasn't working. So I asked her to share how she believes the CFO experiences her and why. "He probably experiences me as too relaxed and accommodating, which might be frustrating given the company's poor financial results. But I like to keep everyone calm and work through the challenges in a supportive way," she says. Once Mary understood how her CFO was experiencing her, we could identify ways she might engage differently to manage his experience. For Mary, this included meeting with her CFO, sharing her observations, and discussing what they could do to build their relationship.

While other awareness is understanding another person's feelings, thoughts, and behaviors, organizational awareness is learning to see ourselves, our relationships, and our work environment through another person's eyes. Organizational awareness is the knowledge you build about how your organization perceives you. We need organizational awareness to know how to work together. For example, a 2012 study published in *The Oxford Handbook of Positive Organizational Scholarship* found that when people who work in different locations make time to meet via Zoom or email to check in (i.e., find out how people are, what they are struggling with, and if they have any feedback), it increases the overall team's coordination and cooperation. When we lack organizational awareness, we don't take the time to understand how our colleagues experience us. This means we are much less likely to make any much-needed adjustments to our behavior to maintain the relationship.

When I worked in human resources for a global multinational organization in the energy and resource sector, one of my jobs required me to spend equal amounts of time working in the London office in England and the Perth office in Australia. I also had to make frequent trips to the Houston office in Texas. Every time I traveled to one of these locations, I would observe the little differences. For example, in the Houston office, employees start work no later than 8:00 a.m. (often as early as 6:00 a.m.) and finish at around 4:00 p.m., often taking a lunch break at 11:00 a.m. In London, employees would start late (sometimes as late as 10:00 a.m.) and finish work by 8:00 p.m.

I would also hear colleagues share their different experiences working with people in other office locations. For example, colleagues in the Houston office believed colleagues in the London office were not very productive or efficient because they worked later hours and often spent a lot of time socializing at the pub after work, even though in London, going to the pub is a common way for teams to socialize and bond. Houston didn't understand the workplace norms regarding working hours in London. Houston's frustrations and miscommunications were born out of misunderstandings and assumptions. For example, the human resources team in the Houston office found the London team to be vague and unclear, which makes sense as research has found that, on average, British people tend to communicate more indirectly, preferring that people infer what they are trying to say. The Houston team also struggled with the Australian team's laid-back and informal approach to managing projects and deadlines. The Australian team's relaxed approach was a way of building relationships and camaraderie, which they saw as critical to achieving deadlines. I shared my awareness of how the other offices operated with my coworkers (in each of the offices). I also explained to each office how colleagues in other locations experienced working with each of them. The more people understood the norms, routines, and perspectives of the other offices and how different offices perceived them, the easier it was for everyone to work together.

Organizational Awareness Enables Collaboration

For a long time, doing a good job was about completing tasks on time and specification—often on your own. Maybe you needed to work with others to do this, but your output ultimately measured your performance. The world of work has changed. Today, collaboration is king. A 2017 Gartner survey found that 67 percent of organizations rank collaboration as the most critical workforce skill and 82 percent report their employees must work closely with colleagues to achieve objectives, including spending time on collaborative activities, phone calls, Zoom meetings, emails, or in-person meetings. Furthermore, a 2021 research study published in *Harvard Business Review* found that ten years ago, collaboration was one-third as crucial as it is today. Remote working has increased how much time we spend collaborating, as employees must overcome the challenges of working together in a virtual environment. Misunderstandings arise at work, especially in a virtual environment, because we have reduced knowledge about the people we work with, their context, and how they perceive us. To avoid misunderstandings, we need to take another person's perspective and understand their world and how they perceive everyone else because this is how we bridge our cultural or demographic differences. When you have organizational awareness, you know why people engage with you the way they do, preventing you from getting offended or taking things the wrong way.

Helping those three offices build their other and organizational awareness ultimately made my job easier. Colleagues in each office became more aware of the working hours in each location, which made it easier for them to find times they were all online. All teams understood how their communication styles were perceived and the impact this had, so they adjusted their approach. The London team started communicating more explicitly in team meetings, and the Houston team knew to ask if they were unsure what was being said or asked of them. Both the London and Houston teams understood the importance of building relationships and set aside time each week to meet and check in with their Australian counterparts even if there were no agenda items. As the teams built their organizational awareness, they came to know why people do what they do and how they perceive one another and their work environment, which made it easier to collaborate.

Building self, other, and organizational awareness is the basis for knowing how to work with others.

We learn to read the air by sharing informal information about ourselves, others, and our work environment. Developing self-awareness is a prerequisite to developing other and organizational awareness. After all, it's tough to understand other people if you don't understand yourself.

Likewise, learning how others think and feel enables us to understand why people do what they do. Knowing who you can ask for information on corporate life's inner workings—when there will be a job opening, restructure, or leadership change—is essential for reading your workplace.

Through self-awareness and other awareness, we build up our organizational awareness, which is the most critical factor for responding to changes at work, like starting a new job or project. Organizational awareness improves communication, culture, and leadership effectiveness. People with organizational awareness can use this information to manage how they are perceived—which benefits them and the people they work with.

Mind the Self-Awareness Gap: Why Reading the Air Matters

One of my first jobs out of university was as an industrial-organizational psychologist administering personality tests, like the Myers-Briggs Type Indicator (MBTI). These tools provide a snapshot of your personality compared to other people. For example, the MBTI will tell you how extroverted or introverted you are compared to the general population. Since the 1960s, it is estimated that over fifty million people have taken the MBTI. We love learning about ourselves. However, while it is interesting to understand your personality type or behavioral preferences, it doesn't change your effectiveness at work.

If you have taken a personality assessment, you know that simply learning about your personality preferences doesn't fundamentally change how you behave at work. One of the reasons for this is that self-ratings of performance are notoriously poor predictors of actual performance. Just because you see yourself a certain way doesn't mean everyone else does. And without knowing how others perceive you, it's impossible to know if your behavior has a positive or negative impact.

For most people, a gap exists between how they see themselves and how others see them—what I refer to as the self-awareness gap. This gap exists because we are not objective. We have an innate need to maintain a positive self-image; without this, recovering from a setback or misstep would be tough. Self-ratings of performance are filtered through this biased self-perception. Generally, research finds a lack of agreement between how we rate ourselves in terms of our behavior and performance and how others rate us. Specifically, a 2018 study in *Harvard Business Review* titled *Working with People Who Aren't Self-Aware* finds that although 95 percent of people think they are self-aware, only about 15 percent are. Of course, we know that other people are not self-aware, as 99 percent of participants reported working with at least one person who isn't self-aware. But most of us don't believe we are this one person, which is a common bias!

When people misdiagnose their strengths and weaknesses, they are unaware of how others perceive them, making them difficult to work with. When I used to administer personality assessments, I often heard other psychologists discuss the personality profiles of the people they were assessing. People were classified as either "nice but not capable" or "competent but a bit of a jerk"—there was no in-between. We like using these labels because they help to simplify things. A competent jerk will do a good job, but they are challenging to work with. A nice person is easy to work with, but people don't think they are capable. But what about a third option—a competent person who is easy to work with?

Research has found people generally fall into one of three categories when it comes to self-awareness. Some people overestimate their capabilities and performance relative to how others see them—the competent jerks. Other people underestimate their capabilities and performance relative to how others see them—the nice person who others think isn't competent. And then there are some people whose self-ratings of capability and performance agree with other people's ratings—these are the self-aware people.

Overestimators

Overestimators are individuals with the qualifications, experience, and intelligence to succeed, but they never seem to make it to the corner office. And if overestimators make it, they don't last long because they are challenging to work with. Overestimators often don't succeed because they are only willing to accept positive feedback. They don't take time to consider different perspectives or reflect on how other people might perceive them. Instead, they simply reject any developmental feedback by blaming others for it. In doing so, they overvalue their contributions and undervalue their teammates.

Overestimators are not open to self-improvement and may come across as arrogant—it's their way or the highway. When competent jerks don't accept feedback, they don't take accountability for the impact their behavior has on others. For example, they can be hurtful without knowing it, and when they do know it, they dismiss other people's feelings or refuse to adjust their approach. Their lack of self-awareness detrimentally impacts coworkers' stress, motivation, and engagement at work. For example, a 2015 *Harvard Business Review* study found that when a team includes one member who is an over-estimator, their chances of success are cut by 50 percent because overestimators make poor decisions, coordinate less, and have poor conflict management.

Not only are overestimators hard to like, but they are also difficult to trust. When people aren't open to feedback and dismiss the impact of their behavior, they are not acting in the best interests of the people around them, making them untrustworthy. Overestimators cannot recognize and appreciate how their perspective differs from another person's. They don't understand the gap because they don't see it. They believe their experience is the only experience of working life.

Unfortunately, self-awareness doesn't improve on its own or with more experience. Research has found the more experienced managers become, the less they can accurately assess their leadership effectiveness. In academia, this phenomenon is known as *the CEO disease* because the more powerful leaders are, the more likely they are to overestimate their performance because people are often afraid to tell them. Employees also don't have many opportunities to provide their CEO with honest feedback about their performance. How many CEOs do you know who provide employees with opportunities to meet one-on-one and provide feedback? For this reason, research has shown that 80 percent of senior executives lack awareness of their skills and 40 percent have strengths they are unaware of and don't utilize.

What separates a top-performing CEO from a mediocre one is self-awareness. There is a strong link between a leader's self-awareness and a company's revenue, profitability, and competitive advantage. But when we only see ourselves as highly experienced leaders or top performers, we are not open to evidence or feedback that might conflict with this self-image. So we disregard negative feedback and refuse to question our assumptions, beliefs, or perspectives, creating false confidence in our performance.

Underestimators

By contrast, underestimators may struggle to diagnose their strengths and lack the confidence to succeed. Even when an underestimator does a good job, they are more likely to overestimate their teammates' contributions and underestimate their own. These people might be capable, but their lack of confidence in their capability is perceived as incompetence. It's hard to believe someone can do a job if they don't believe it. One of the reasons for this is that we mistake displays of confidence for competence. The more self-assured, assertive, and outspoken someone is, the more likely we are to believe they know what they are doing—it's why so many business people will advise new hires or graduates entering the workforce to "fake it till you make it." This advice is risky because if you form fake beliefs about yourself and believe this biased self-talk, you risk becoming an overestimator who is much less likely to succeed in the long run.

However, underestimators can develop their self-awareness because they are open to feedback and willing to adjust their behavior. With enough support, coaching, and feedback, they can start to see their strengths and understand their value.

The ideal, though, is to have a high degree of self-awareness, which is the alignment between how you see yourself—when it comes to your behavior, thoughts, and feelings—and how others see you. A competent person who is easy to work with is typically someone who is self-aware. Overall, research has found the more self-aware you are, the more likely you are to make better decisions, lead effectively, and perform better at your tasks. For example, a 2015 study published in the *European Journal of Training and Development* found that self-awareness positively correlates with job-related well-being, appreciation of diversity, improved communication, and confidence at work. The same is true regarding team performance: a 2019 research study published in the *Journal of Management* examined 515 teams and found when teams included individuals with a high level of self-awareness, the team had more effective collaboration and a higher level of performance overall.

Self-awareness is also the key to unlocking creativity. Research has found that self-awareness enables creativity because you have to be open to other people's feedback to develop innovations, products, and services. To create, we must carefully consider different ideas and perspectives and evaluate this information to decide what feedback to incorporate. Most creative achievements involve a painful revision process of incorporating feedback. While appreciated, I have lost count of how many times the manuscript for this book was edited! But every edit built my awareness of what aspects of my writing still need improvement. Every edit improved the quality of the manuscript and my writing. Inviting others to review your ideas, evaluate your work in progress, and provide input and suggestions enables you to innovate, problem-solve, and create.

It's also a determinant of organizational success. Research by the consulting firm Korn Ferry found that companies with poor financial performance are 79 percent more likely to have employees with low self-awareness than companies with high financial performance. This study also found that high-performing employees with long-term career success are more self-aware. Self-aware people are more successful because they are easy to work with *because* they seek out informal information to know if a (self-awareness) gap exists in how they are perceived and what they need to do to close it.

Informal Information Sharing: Three Practices to Close the Self-Awareness Gap

Early in my career, I coached and advised Brendan, a senior manager in corporate finance. In just a few years, Brendan was promoted to chief financial officer, and it was rumored he was in line to become the next CEO. I sat opposite Brendan, so I would observe how he worked every day. Brendan didn't work excessive hours, but I noticed he spent a lot of time on the phone, in meetings, and generally chatting with people in the office.

I asked Brendan if he ever got tired of talking to people.

"Yes, of course. I'm an introvert. But it's my job to know what people around the table are saying," he said.

Brendan was so successful because he knew how others were thinking and feeling. He understood the different challenges they faced. He provided informal advice, support, and information to his teammates. He checked in with his boss and looked for ways to be helpful. He understood the business because he understood the people in it. Importantly, he knew how people perceived him. So all the time he spent with other people was an investment in closing the gap.

Closing the self-awareness gap should not be a onetime effort; instead, it must become a habit. You need to know the practices that will help you access the informal information needed to build your self-awareness, other awareness, and organizational awareness.

Practice 1: Reflect, Review, Regulate: Cycle Through Self-Awareness

Self-awareness isn't created in isolation. Learning to read what people around the table think about you is a dynamic process. Brendan was constantly seeking out information on how others perceived him. For example, at least once a week, Brendan would check in with me and ask me to share my opinions, ideas, and advice on just about anything—like managing team conflicts, business decisions, staff morale issues, and his personal development. Brendan knew he couldn't achieve his ambitions if others were not supportive. He had to focus on managing how he achieved his goals, and he did this by asking for feedback, taking time to get to know his peers, and supporting and energizing them. Whenever Brendan reached out to ask for my input on his approach, he collected another piece of informal information that he could use to understand how I perceived him and how I thought he should approach different situations.

Self-awareness is a dynamic, continuous cycle of *reflecting* on who you are and how you think you come across to others, seeking out clues or evidence that might contradict this, and *reviewing* this information to decide how to *regulate* your behavior so you come across in the way you want. So the cycle of self-awareness then includes three things: reflect, review, and regulate.

Reflect

Reflection is the practice of thinking about your behaviors, thoughts, and feelings and the impact they have on other people. For example, think about a difficult situation you encountered at work, like when you were frustrated or angry with a decision. What were your actions in this situation? Did you raise your voice, sigh, or roll your eyes? What were you feeling and thinking? How did your emotional reaction influence your behavior? How did your response affect how other people responded? While you might have thought your behavior was a proportionate response to the decision, what evidence is there that other people believed this to be the case?

Research published in the 2018 *Harvard Business Review* article titled "What Self-Awareness Really Is (and How to Cultivate It)" found that simply understanding how you think, feel, and behave isn't enough to build self-awareness. Like knowing your personality type, introspection doesn't build self-awareness. People in this study who asked themselves *why* questions—like *why don't I like my job?*, *why don't I get along with my boss?*, or *why don't I agree with a decision at work?*—were less self-aware. Just like taking a personality test, simply knowing why we do what we do isn't enough to build self-awareness.

When individuals reflect on why they do what they do, they are less self-aware because they are simply examining their own beliefs—like why they believe what they do. They are not looking for evidence to challenge those beliefs. For example, what evidence is there that you may lack the skills needed to do your job? Are you difficult to manage? If so, how do you know? What evidence is there that you are not good enough? When we ask *why* questions, we come up with answers based on our fears, insecurities, biases, and beliefs—like *I don't like my boss or coworkers because they are difficult to work with*. To be self-aware, we must reflect on *what* questions, not *why* questions. *What* would it take to enjoy a job, work well with your boss, and agree on an important decision at work? When we ask *what* questions, we seek evidence and feedback on where the gap lies and what we need to do to close it.

In another *Harvard Business Review* study, researchers found that employees working in a call center who spent fifteen minutes a day reflecting on what happened and what they could do better increased their performance (as rated by customers) by 23 percent within ten days compared to employees who didn't take time to reflect. When we make reflection a regular practice, it doesn't only improve performance. Research has also found that regular reflection at work is associated with higher job satisfaction, improved decision-making, positive feelings, enhanced well-being, and reduced anxiety and depression.

Reflecting is as simple as taking a few minutes each day to think about what you did at work and how you did it. This includes considering *what* you could do to improve rather than spending hours examining *why* you do what you do.

Review

While reflection is the process of going inward to understand how you work and what you could do to improve, reviewing is the process of considering how other people perceive your performance. The aim of reviewing is to gather as much informal information, like feedback or different perspectives on your performance, as possible to review if a gap exists between how others see you and how you see yourself. The aim of reviewing is to be able to decide what, if anything, you might need to do to close the gap.

While reflection is something we can do on our own, reviewing ourselves requires input from others, which is difficult as most of our work might not be evident to others. In fact, many of the tasks we undertake at work are invisible to others. No one watches us write a report, perform an analysis, or create a presentation at work. Even if there is a physical manifestation of your work, like an Excel sheet, there might be very few coworkers around to see how you create it or who you work with. A 2014 research study published in *Information Systems Research* found that work is becoming increasingly invisible, as there are fewer and fewer tasks people undertake that can be physically observed. You probably don't see what tasks your coworkers are undertaking or how they undertake them. At the same time, most of your coworkers probably don't know what tasks you are performing and how you undertake them. In hybrid workplaces, coworkers are simply unaware of what their teammates are working on and how they do it. This reduced work visibility increases the duplication of tasks and reduces trust, coordination, innovation, peer-to-peer learning, and cooperation. But ultimately, a lack of visibility hurts us because it reduces self-awareness.

You need input from your teammates to know if a self-awareness gap exists and what you need to do to close it. You need to know how they perceive both what you are doing and how you are doing it. This can be as simple as taking a few minutes between each task to reflect on what was accomplished and ask people what impact it had. For example, when I facilitate leadership development programs as part of my consultancy business, I build in a few minutes throughout the session to check in. I ask my cofacilitators and attendees for feedback. Are we going too fast? Does the content make sense? Do people have any questions about what was covered? What can we do to support everyone? These check-ins create opportunities for people to let me know how they perceive the session so I know what adjustments to make.

Reviewing is the practice of evaluating your performance. Most people wait until their formal quarterly or annual performance review for their manager to decide how they are progressing—but by this point, it is too late to make any improvements. Once you have reflected on what you would like to improve, the only way you know if you are making progress is to evaluate yourself. This means taking a few minutes each week to review what you achieved and how you achieved it to see where you've made progress and where you have fallen short. You can then test your self-assessment against how other people view your performance to see if any gaps exist. This can be as simple as asking people to evaluate a piece of work you delivered or how you managed the team to deliver a project.

The aim of reviewing yourself is to identify any gaps in your self-awareness. A self-aware person like Brendan knows where the gap exists between how they see themselves and how others see them—because they take time to review the evidence. Therefore, they don't rely solely on their self-evaluation. Instead, they seek out information that might provide clues as to how others see them and what they need to do to close any gaps. By regularly reviewing your performance and including other people's evaluations in your overall assessment, you will know what adjustments you need to make. This is how you can close the gap so that there are no surprises when your annual performance review comes around!

Regulate

Most of us hate having our performance evaluated. We worry that other people might perceive us in a negative light. In fact, according to a survey of Fortune 1000 companies undertaken by the corporate executive board, 66 percent of employees were strongly dissatisfied with their performance evaluations. One of the reasons performance reviews are unhelpful is that they happen only a few times a year. By the time a person receives input into how they could have approached a situation differently, the moment has passed. Performance evaluations only work if they happen all the time. Fortunately, we don't have to wait for our managers to do this. If you, like Brendan, regularly review how you work, you will know what self-awareness gaps might exist. And you can close these gaps by regulating your behavior.

Regulating is the practice of adjusting our behavior at work to ensure it positively impacts the people we work with.

The final step in the self-awareness cycle is to adjust your behavior to close the gap. In Brendan's example, he knew that people felt he tended to micromanage, especially when it came time to finalize the annual company report, which is a shareholder document that outlines the company's annual performance. Brendan was accountable for pulling the document together. So, to adjust his approach, Brendan checked in with his team to ask how they would prefer to be managed; he practiced delegating by setting clear expectations, providing regular feedback, and trying to let go of perfectionism. Research has shown that greater self-awareness is associated with improved self-regulated behavior, psychological well-being, and mental health. When you reflect on your performance and obtain evaluations from others, you know where the gap exists and what to do to manage it. Self-awareness is the art of regulating your behavior to manage gaps in how you see yourself and others perceive you. The 2015 *Harvard Business Review* article titled "We're Not Very Self-Aware, Especially at Work" found that we like working with people who react positively to feedback and make the necessary changes to their behavior. Responsiveness shows you care, and people can trust you to behave in a way that has their best interests in mind. Once you know what you need to change, your only job left is to change it.

Practice 2: Build Other Awareness Through the Practice of Perspective-Taking

Using your index finger, take a minute to draw the letter E on your forehead. Did you write the letter E facing your direction—so you could read it? Or did you write it facing the right way for someone else to read? A 2004 study published in the *Journal of Social and Clinical Psychology* found that when people were asked to draw an *E* on their foreheads, more self-aware people would draw the *E* from the perspective of the other person rather than themselves. Just like if you were to guide a person through a maze, you would tell them to turn right or left based on their perspective, not your right or left. The more self-aware you are, the fewer errors you will make when directing others.

Perspective-taking is the practice of considering how another person might think, feel, and behave and why. Perspective-taking enhances empathy because, without it, you are likely to want to use people for how they can support your ambitions regardless of the personal cost to them. However, perspective-taking goes beyond empathy, which recognizes how a person might feel, to recognizing why someone is doing what they are doing, i.e., what they might be thinking and how this is informing their behavior.

When we don't engage in perspective-taking, we tend to rely on snap judgments to guide our interactions. Research has found that it takes less than one-tenth of a second to form an assessment of a person. We look at a person and decide in a few seconds if they are competent, likable, warm, supportive, and easy to work with. Our impressions are not random; they are based on our experiences, beliefs, and biases. We make snapshot judgments about whether a person is warm, supportive, and easy to work with based on their physical appearance and nonverbal behavior like gestures, eye contact, and facial expressions. These judgments don't change with time. In fact, when people have longer to form an initial impression of another person, they tend to be more confident that it is correct, even though it isn't.

Snap judgments are often wrong because they lack context—they don't account for why people think, feel, and behave in the way they do. However, when we engage in perspective-taking, we are more likely to be able to interpret accurately how other people think, feel, and behave. For example, when the pandemic hit, my children's school closed. Like many dual-income families, my husband and I juggled homeschooling with full-time jobs. Often I would switch my camera off because I didn't want my children to distract my coworkers. I received feedback from a senior leader in the company I was working for that I didn't seem that committed or engaged and needed to be more present in meetings. But had he engaged in perspective-taking, he would have understood how hard I was trying to remain present and engaged—despite homeschooling two children under six years of age! The more accurate our assessments are of why people think, feel, and behave in the way they do, the better we are placed to respond with empathy, care, and understanding.

Research has found when individuals engage in perspective-taking, it increases their awareness of themselves and others, improving their relationships. For example, Menlo Innovations is a small software design company based in Michigan that relies on computer programmers to work together to develop software. The company ensures coworkers collaborate by building other awareness through perspective-taking. Every day at 10:00 a.m., the programmers stand in a circle and provide one another with a short update on their work. Everyone is invited to share information related to their challenges, concerns, and approaches to work. Other people are encouraged to listen with empathy and consider that person's perspective. Then they can offer advice, assistance, and gratitude for their teammate's efforts. The aim isn't just to make people more aware of what everyone is doing and why. Rather the goal is to help teammates engage in the norm of reciprocity by understanding one another's perspectives and then offering support, appreciation, and reassurance to build stronger connections and enhance collaboration.

A lack of self and other awareness damages individual and team performance. For example, think about a person on your team who does the bare minimum—what academics refer to as a *social loafer*. Often social loafers are unaware that other people notice they are slacking off. The more team members notice a person is slacking off, the less likely they are to interact with them or expect any contribution from them. Over time, the lack of engagement disconnects the social loafer from the group. The only way to break this cycle is for the social loafer to realize how they are behaving and the impact it is having (self-awareness), and why other people are not engaging with them (other awareness).

Anyone can engage in perspective-taking to enhance their self- and other awareness. When it comes to practicing perspective-taking, people often assume it is as simple as imagining how the other person might feel. So if you were working on a team with a social loafer, you might think about how the social loafer feels in response to their colleagues icing them out. But this is not as effective as imagining yourself as the social loafer. When we imagine ourselves in the other person's situation, how they feel and think or why they behave as they do, we more accurately understand their perspective.

While the most accurate way to tell how another person thinks or feels is to ask them, often this can be difficult as people might not be comfortable sharing or lack the self-awareness to know the answer. You can, however, engage in perspective-taking by imagining yourself in a similar situation to the other person. If we think about the social loafer example, you could engage in perspective-taking by taking on the role of the social loafer and *considering what they think and feel and why.* Why are you not contributing to the team's activities? Do you feel excluded? Do you even know what you are expected to contribute? How are you as the social loafer experiencing the team, and how is this contributing to your choices? Then *consider what the other person needs to change their behavior.* In this case, what do you, the social loafer, need to contribute to the group task? It's helpful to consider a similar experience you might have had, like a time when you felt excluded or unsure of the expectations people had of you. What did you need to feel comfortable engaging or contributing? Finally, *consider what your response (as the social loafer) would be if people offered to meet those needs.* How would you respond if team members reached out to make sure you felt included and to share what they needed from you?

When people make it a habit to engage in perspective-taking, it improves individual and team performance. Perspective-taking ensures you are not indifferent to someone else's suffering. Instead, you understand the impact your behaviors have on others and the impact other people's behaviors have on your team. The more you can see the other person's perspective and engage in behavior that supports them (following the norm of reciprocity), the more likely they will support you.

Practice 3: Share Reflected Knowledge to Build Organizational Awareness

Brendan had a knack for making people feel understood. He would meet with people to find out what they were working on, what they needed, and if there was anything that wasn't working for them— and share his perspective in return. The more people reflected their knowledge of the organization back to Brendan, the more he understood how they experienced the organization. And vice versa. To build strong relationships at work, you need other people to feel understood by you.

Reflected knowledge is the informal information people share at work that helps you understand how they perceive the organization, including the dynamics of relationships within a team, individual team members' strengths and weaknesses, team norms, and organizational decisions or challenges. For example, I had reflected knowledge of the London, Houston, and Perth teams because I knew how the offices perceived one another. And I could use this understanding to help each of the teams improve their collaboration. When you understand how your coworkers perceive one another's intentions, needs, behaviors, and context, you can see yourself and the organization through another person's eyes.

When you lack organizational awareness, you make poor decisions because you have not considered all the facts and are not in touch with what people think or feel.

Organizational awareness depends on people's willingness to share their reflections. Unfortunately, many people wrongly believe (as the old saying goes) that knowledge is power. Consequently, people often hoard information because they want to feel like they have something other people don't. But in practice, the old adage isn't true because sharing our reflected knowledge is how we build organizational awareness. We make it safe for other people to share their insights with us when we trust them with ours. How much we trust someone determines how likely we are to work with them or offer support with a complicated issue and help them succeed.

Sharing reflected knowledge is how we demonstrate trust. When you trust people, you are more likely to let people in and share your reflections about how you perceive the organization. To collaborate in person or virtually, we must trust one another, which means we must create mutual understanding. We need to understand the other person's intentions, needs, and behaviors. When you take time to understand other people's perspectives, you demonstrate your willingness to act with other people's interests in mind, making you trustworthy. The more someone feels understood by you, research finds, the more they will trust you. Moreover, when you are confident other people understand your motivations, you are more likely to be perceived as trustworthy.

To build organizational awareness, we must make sharing reflected knowledge a practice by making time (like Brendan) to meet with coworkers and share our experiences of the organization. The challenge with sharing reflected knowledge is people often mistake this practice for gossiping, which includes sharing informal information to advance a personal agenda. But building organizational awareness is more about demonstrating that you care about your coworkers by paying attention to them, valuing their contributions, understanding their challenges, and listening to their needs. Consider how often you demonstrate the following behaviors to know if you are building your organizational awareness by sharing your reflected knowledge.

- You take time to listen to your coworkers and consider their different opinions or points of view.
- You pay attention to other people's needs and demonstrate a genuine interest in your coworkers' ambitions, goals, and work or career advancement.
- You recognize the contributions and effort of your teammates.
- You can articulate how valuable each of your coworkers is and the unique attributes they bring to the team.

Taking time to listen to your coworkers and understand their challenges ensures people want to be around you and contribute to your success because you are investing in their growth and development by helping them solve challenges or share their difficulties at work. The relationship is mutually beneficial, so it is essential to balance the time you spend sharing your reflections with capturing other people's viewpoints. One way to know if you are investing enough time in sharing your reflected knowledge is to think about an important decision that has been made in your organization, like a leadership change, downsizing, or not going ahead with a particular project. Then think about the people involved in the decision. Did you understand their perspectives regarding the challenges, opportunities, or costs the decision might create for them? The more you know how your coworkers experience the organization when it comes to difficult decisions, the less uncertainty you will have about how they are likely to respond to those future challenges. When you know how your coworkers are likely to behave, you know how you need to respond to work with them. And likewise, if they know how you are likely to respond, they will know how to work with you.

Don't Fake It Till You Make It

The old saying "fake it till you make it" encourages people to pretend to think, feel, and behave in a confident, outgoing, and assertive way even though this isn't how they really feel. The hope is that if you act one way, your feelings and thoughts will eventually catch up. But faking it requires a lot of mental and emotional effort. It's stressful to pretend to be someone else. Or hide how you think and feel because you are never sure if someone will eventually call you out. People who fake it are often considered social chameleons because they build a public self-image that matches who other people want them to be. They actively monitor and control their self-expression in social situations by carefully choosing their words, tone, dress, and gestures. These individuals often fake their interest in others and may be perceived as disingenuous. The challenge is that they don't behave consistently or predictably, making them hard to trust.

On the other hand, people who are consistent in their behavior are easy to trust. The challenge is that often these individuals disregard how their thoughts, feelings, and actions make other people feel. Often you will hear these people say, "I am who I am, and I won't change for anyone." The challenge with this approach is that it is inherently selfish. When you are unwilling to adjust your approach to manage the impact it has on other people, what you are really saying is you don't care. But being your authentic self isn't simply saying, *This is who I am; take it or leave it*. It also isn't about faking it. Being authentic is about being self-, other-, and organizationally aware.

When you behave authentically, your actions are guided by what you value, believe, think, and feel. Research finds that behaving in a consistent, predictable way aligned with what you believe and value increases your self-esteem and emotional well-being and reduces your anxiety and depression. Importantly, though, this consistently includes valuing how other people experience you. That means accounting for the impact your actions have on other people. Self-aware people don't distort, exaggerate, or ignore informal information that might inform their self-development. Instead, they actively gather and share informal information to build their awareness. The aim is to identify gaps in how their behaviors are perceived so they know what to do to close these gaps.

5

INFORMAL DEVELOPMENT

How We Learn to Read the Air

Sitting in a small, dusty, windowless office in Houston, Texas, I am wondering if Shaun, an online recruitment software company CEO, will be able to keep his job. Shaun looks like a typical CEO. He is white, middle-class, heterosexual, highly educated, able-bodied, and male. For the last twenty-four months, I have been coaching Shaun to help him become more inclusive, empathic, and caring.

Shaun started his career as a software developer and is now running a business about to be listed on the New York Stock Exchange. His company has grown quickly, and while he has all the technical skills needed to do the job of a CEO, Shaun struggles with people. Results from the annual employee survey reveal that employees don't feel included, supported, valued, or connected to the organization, and many are thinking about leaving. The board has given Shaun twelve months to turn these results around. The only problem is Shaun lacks the know-how to do this. Most of the feedback Shaun has received reveals one consistent theme: he focuses on what he achieves at the expense of managing how he works with others.

I stare at the books on the shelf behind him. Nearly all the books are technical manuals and how-to guides from training courses Shaun has completed. But Shaun doesn't need to develop any more technical skills. He has a whole team of technical experts. His job is to lead. To do this, Shaun has to learn how to motivate people, support their development, and build relationships with globally diverse teams, all of which require the ability to read the air. There is no training course for this; it's something Shaun will have to learn on the job.

In many ways, Shaun represents a lot of leaders today. Take a few minutes and close your eyes. I want you to picture what an ideal competent leader looks like in your workplace. What are their demographic characteristics? How do they speak? How do they behave? Are they task-focused? Dominant and assertive? Do they tell employees what to do, with employees largely following suit? Or are they democratic, caring, inclusive, and supportive? Do they focus on people over policies or processes? The *ideal worker* is an academic term used to describe people's shared mental image of what *good* looks like when it comes to competence and leadership. The ideal worker is the shared mental image we all have of the behaviors we all need to engage in to succeed at work.

While the ideal worker might look a little different in every workplace, industry, or country, research over the last thirty years (conducted by leading organizational psychologist Dr. Virginia E. Schein) has found that employees' perceptions of the ideal worker are pretty consistent. For most individuals, the ideal worker is someone who looks a lot like Shaun—that is, typically white and male. Importantly, my own research has found that not only is the ideal worker someone who engages in dominant, assertive, aggressive, and competitive behavior, but they are also willing to work long hours, engage in exclusionary behavior, and discriminate against others to maintain their dominant position at work and advance their careers. Engaging in these behaviors is how people advance individual achievement—often at the expense of their coworkers.

This ideal worker exists because our idea of what good looks like at work was formed during the industrial era—where most companies focused on productivity at all costs, relying on a hierarchical, transactional approach to work. The shift from an industrial economy (where most people worked in factories) to the information economy we have now (where most people work in an office) has created a shift in ideal worker behaviors.

Companies focused on automation and mass production in the industrial economy. Most individuals would stand in an assembly line in a factory and complete the same task over and over. Maximizing your individual productivity was what mattered most. You only needed manual or technical skills that could be taught—what we call hard skills. But today, in the information economy, where knowledge and information are more valuable than manufacturing, technical or job-specific skills (often referred to as hard skills) are not enough to get ahead—especially in the age of automation. In an office environment, employees must focus on what they produce and, more important, how they produce it. Consequently, employees need advanced social and emotional skills (often referred to as soft skills) to demonstrate emotional intelligence, inclusion, collaboration, critical thinking, flexibility, adaptability, authenticity, and resilience. In the 1960s, the United States military invented the term *soft skills* to differentiate social skills from the technical skills people had to develop to work with machines. While the term *soft skills* was never meant to refer to these skills in a derogatory way, most people associate the word *soft* as being unnecessary or noncritical, which couldn't be further from the truth. Soft skills are really what I call *universal skills*, because most employees will require these skills to work in any role and for any employer.

Developing hard skills helps employees deliver on the *what* of work—what we are making, what we are selling, what we are working on in a production line. But universal skills help employees manage the *how* of work—how we are making, selling, and collaborating. Research published in *Harvard Business Review* found that across all employment levels today, more and more jobs require greater social skills, like the ability to persuade, include, and collaborate with others. These types of jobs grow at a faster rate, and the compensation for them also grows faster than the average.

Although there is a huge demand for technological expertise like information technology and programming capabilities—job categories that are expected to grow as much as 90 percent between 2016 and 2030—not everyone will need these advanced technical capabilities. Instead, most of us will need basic digital skills, like computer literacy and web-based research, which we can develop through traditional learning formats or formal training programs provided at work. As I've noted, as workplaces become more informal, ambiguous, and volatile, we will need to develop our universal skills, like social and emotional competencies, to know how to work together to maximize our collective productivity. Research has found that 75 percent of long-term job success depends on soft skills, and only 25 percent depends on technical capabilities. Additionally, employers rate soft skills as the most critical factor for entry-level success on the job.

The challenge today is that most of us—much like Shaun—are suffering from an ideal worker hangover because we value and engage in behaviors that no longer serve us. Most leaders engage in behaviors that were once viewed as normal but are now considered counterproductive—like relying on hierarchy or positional power to influence others and adopting a command-and-control approach to decision-making. An *MIT Sloan Management Review* survey of

4,393 individuals from more than 120 countries found that only 12 percent of respondents strongly agree that their leaders have the right mindsets to lead them forward. Engaging in outdated ideal worker behaviors costs leaders like Shaun because no one wants to work with or for them. Shaun is exceptionally knowledgeable and hardworking, but his interactions with his leadership team are abrupt, direct, and uncaring. In just one year, more than half of Shaun's leadership team quit because they didn't enjoy their work experience.

Also, we might not even realize how engaging in old ideal worker behaviors reduces our ability to get our work done. Research by Catalyst in 2010 found that adhering to outdated ways of working hinders individual and organizational performance. For example, Shaun's company had nearly doubled in head count and productivity within a few short years at the expense of building an inclusive, collaborative culture. Consequently, the company could not attract and retain talent, which in recent months had stalled the company's growth. Workplaces simply don't acknowledge that the ideal worker behaviors employees and leaders still engage in are not the behaviors they need now or in the future.

But beyond developing advanced universal skills, we need to know how to apply them at work. It isn't enough to be an inclusive person in your personal life. To be inclusive at work, you need to know how to practice this universal skill when it comes to informal networking, information sharing, and supporting your teammates' development and advancement.

In the industrial era—the old world of work—success was synonymous with having *power over others*. To be considered influential, you would have to dominate and control others, like telling teammates when a lunch break could be taken or writing someone up for tardiness. The more you could micromanage and bark orders at people to get them to follow you, the more likely you would be seen as a potential leader. Excluding or devaluing people was a way to maintain power. So, too, was hoarding important information and only sharing it with a select few. Success at any cost—to people or the environment—was considered an acceptable business practice.

For example, when it comes to the four informal systems of work—networks, information sharing, development, and advancement—the old ideal worker was engaged in the following behaviors:

Informal Networks

- Invest in building relationships with people similar to themselves (in terms of demographic characteristics).
- Exclude coworkers (who are demographically different) from accessing informal networks as a way to preserve power over others.
- Rely on small, closed networks.

Informal Information Sharing

- Hoard informal information to maintain power. This includes withholding important information or sharing it selectively.
- Exclude people who are different (from them) by not sharing important information.

Informal Development Opportunities

- Wait for informal development opportunities to be provided by leaders who favor them within the organization.
- Access informal coaching and mentoring by fitting the old ideal worker standard.

Informal Advancement Opportunities
- Obtain advancement opportunities by fitting the old ideal worker standard and focusing on what you deliver (often at the expense of how).
- Focus on individual achievement at all costs.

But the new world of work has created new unwritten rules, which reflect the new definition of success. It's no longer about having power *over* others but rather power *with* others, which is about working with others to achieve results. In the new world of work, we must learn how to bridge our differences with others so we can collaborate, innovate, and solve complex problems. Importantly, this means working with people who don't share your background or identity. This includes building diverse informal networks, sharing informal information, and supporting our coworkers' development and advancement. *Power with* is about reciprocity—recognizing that individual success depends on our collective ability to work together. Achieving anything depends on your ability to focus on *what* you do and *how* you do it. Therefore, your ability to manage *how* you work is your path to power.

For example, when it comes to the four informal systems of work, the new ideal worker is someone who would engage in the following behaviors:

Informal Networks
- Invest in building relationships with people who are demographically diverse.
- Develop a range of diverse, informal networks with a mix of close relationships and acquaintances.
- Develop relationships that are mutually beneficial.

Informal Information Sharing

- Share informal information to connect with others, build relationships, and support others' development.
- Share informal information with a wide range of people to build self-awareness, other awareness, and organizational awareness.

Informal Development Opportunities

- Seek opportunities to learn both soft and hard skills on the job.
- Access informal development opportunities through peer-to-peer relationships.
- Support their coworkers' development by providing advice, support, and guidance.

Informal Advancement Opportunities

- Actively manage their career advancement rather than relying on an organization for advancement opportunities.
- Focus on collective rather than individual achievement.
- Pay it forward by supporting their coworkers' advancement.

When we join an organization, we watch, often unknowingly, how leaders behave. Over time, we understand what behaviors get rewarded, supported, endorsed, and promoted. These behaviors are the ideal worker behaviors. Without knowing it, we begin to internalize the ideal worker and behave in a way that is aligned with it. This happens because we want to be perceived as competent and leader-like.

The problem is that a lot of us might be following an outdated model and not even know it. Or, much like Shaun, we simply don't know how to learn a new way of working. To put it succinctly, what got you here won't get you any further.

Your Potential Is Your Ability to Learn

Whenever I think about a person's potential, I am reminded of an old Zen parable in which a martial arts student asks his teacher, "I am devoted to studying your martial system. How long will it take me to master it?"

The teacher replies, "Ten years."

Frustrated, the student asks again, "But I want to master it quicker than that. I will work hard and practice every day. How long will it take then?"

The teacher pauses, looking at the student thoughtfully, and he replies, "Twenty years."

Our potential to advance at work isn't determined by how ambitious we are, the number of hours we clock, or the qualifications or technical skills we acquire over the course of our careers. Anyone can work hard or attend a course. But, unfortunately, like the martial arts student, if you believe that hard work is all it takes to get ahead, you might spend years slogging away at a dead-end job, only to find your career has bottomed out.

Companies often sell the idea that an employee's potential is determined by the skills they can list on a résumé, but this isn't true. Just take a look at the way companies promote employees within an organization. Every year, managers will meet to discuss which employees have the potential to move to the next level. Leaders will debate employees' different skill sets to try and achieve consensus on the final list of candidates for future leadership positions. What leaders are assessing isn't the technical or universal skills an employee has; instead, it's their ability to learn on the job.

When you take on a new role at work, you generally have to learn new skills to do the job. According to a 2022 report by McKinsey, when people change jobs, in particular when they move into a higher-paying role, the new job typically involves learning new technical and universal skills that were not required in their previous role. For example, before Shaun took on the CEO role, he was the chief operations officer and oversaw the technical and operational aspects of the business. When Shaun changed his job to CEO, the board shared with him the gaps in his leadership capability that he would need to fill—like learning to be inclusive, democratic, and empathic. Shaun got the CEO position because the board believed he could learn these skills in his new role. In other words, he was promoted because of his potential to learn on the job.

Whenever I recruit people into my organization, I try to find out how much runway—how much potential—they have. By this, I mean their potential to learn new skills, outgrow their job, and move on to something bigger and better. Potential for me is when a person is willing to improve their capabilities, take on new challenges, learn from their failures, and accept feedback. I want to invest my time and energy in growing people who can grow with my business. People who don't want to develop or would like to do the same thing every day will find it challenging to work in my organization. Even if you want to stand still, you can't because workplaces constantly adapt to changes in the broader environment. Your ability to acquire new skills determines how employable you are. The more you can learn, the more skills you will acquire and the more valuable you will be to prospective employers—mainly because you can demonstrate that you know how to learn and grow.

Your potential—the length of your runway—is determined by your willingness to develop new skills and to do so on the job. The ability to learn determines your potential for promotions and your earnings over a lifetime. For example, the 2022 McKinsey study also found that employees who are given access to new opportunities, like new roles or special projects to develop their skills, tend to be offered more and more development opportunities in the future and greater financial rewards. Specifically, the research found that an employee's ability to acquire new skills *on the job* will contribute to almost half of their total wealth. Your ability to learn determines how far you go in your career.

Outside of learning new technical skills, each of us will need to know how to learn to engage in new ideal worker behaviors to get our jobs done. Specifically, we need to learn how to engage in the new ideal worker behaviors when it comes to how we informally network, share information, and access development and promotion opportunities. Potential, then, is really our ability to learn how to read the air.

Shaun has three degrees and numerous technical qualifications. However, his development has almost exclusively focused on hard skills—degrees or technical training. Like most people, Shaun hoped his company would help him develop the soft skills he needed to succeed in his CEO role. Only they didn't. And the bad news for all of us is that most workplaces won't. Largely because you can't learn skills—like reading the air—in a classroom or by taking an e-learning course. Formal learning programs, which include any training provided in a classroom or e-learning format, may be great for developing hard skills, but universal skills are learned informally by observing people, by obtaining informal feedback, or through trial and error. The problem is most of us—like Shaun—don't know how to learn informally, which limits our potential. So the board tasked me with coaching Shaun to think about how he could develop new ways of working and leading because his company was worried he had reached the end of his runway.

That's why there is a growing concern that most of us simply don't have the skills workplaces need, and this skill gap will continue to widen. The World Economic Forum recently declared a "reskilling emergency" because, over the next decade, it is estimated that 1.1 billion jobs will be radically transformed by technology. This will require employees to develop new capabilities, including advanced universal skills. Yet most of us don't believe we have the skills we need to meet the ever-changing world of work. For example, a 2016 Pew Research study found that 54 percent of employees surveyed believe they must continually learn new skills to keep up with changes in their work environment. However, 35 percent of workers (with a bachelor's degree) don't believe they have the education and training needed to get ahead at work. In addition, seven out of ten participants don't rely on their workplace for training and development. Companies in the United States spend around $160 billion yearly on formal learning programs, even though 75 percent of everything we learn is learned informally.

Learning to Read the Air: The Three Practices

Your potential—your ability to learn—is determined by two important things: your intention to learn a new skill and your ability to take ownership of your development. When it comes to developing our universal skills, many of us are unclear about what we want to learn and why. One of the main reasons for this is we are often unaware of the four informal systems that exist in workplaces or how to navigate them—as I shared in chapter three. Your intention to learn a new way of informally networking or building relationships at work determines how much you learn. When we learn informally, by observing people or obtaining informal feedback or trial and error, we take ownership of what we want to develop—we are intentional about it.

But when we learn something incidentally—by default or chance—it doesn't stick. Like when you learn a historical fact by watching a game show on TV but then forget it the next day. Being intentional about what we want to learn requires that we are deliberate in how we go about learning that skill—that is, we take ownership of our development. Specifically, this includes monitoring, planning, and looking for ways to meet your learning needs while undertaking your job. To maximize your potential (your ability to learn continuously), you need to take ownership of what you learn and how you learn it.

And being intentional about your development isn't just about learning a new skill that didn't exist a few years ago. Instead, it's being intentional about learning to read the air and doing this by connecting, supporting, and learning from your teammates. For instance, if you know you want to be more collaborative at work, you might want to understand how effective you are in working with others and what you need to do to change. To get this information, you must practice self-awareness and other awareness, as outlined in chapter four.

To learn to read the air, being intentional matters, but it isn't enough; we must take ownership of our development. That means identifying ways we can informally learn to read the air as part of undertaking our job—by observing others and learning through obtaining feedback or trial and error. Specifically, based on my research, I know the practices for learning how to read the air include becoming *aware* of the unwritten rules, *understanding* how to practice them at work, and then *applying* and refining your ability over time. These three practices—awareness, understanding, and application—reflect the steps people cycle through to learn how to apply the new ideal worker behaviors when navigating informal networks, information sharing, development, and advancement opportunities.

All three practices reinforce one another, so you can't skip one or cherry-pick any. For example, as you become aware of the unwritten rules in your workplace and understand how to apply them in your job, you may start to practice them. However, you will only know if you are successful if you know how people in your workplace respond to your behavior and understand what adjustments you might need to make. The process of learning and mastering *how* you work is continually cycling through your awareness, understanding, and application of the unwritten rules.

Practice 1: Awareness: Learning by Observing

Some people have asked me why I can't simply come up with a long list of potential behaviors that the new ideal worker would engage in and get people to follow that. But this isn't how we learn. Simply outlining a prescriptive list of actions for people to follow never works because every person, interaction, task, job, team, department, and workplace is different. So the trick is not to overwhelm yourself with an exhaustive list of possible actions but for you to identify the most effective way to practice these behaviors in your workplace.

Awareness is the practice of learning by observing. Whether or not you are aware of it, you learn how to read the air by observing how people navigate the four informal systems, why some succeed and why others don't. For example, Catalyst found in 2010 that people who get promoted make it a habit to notice who gets ahead and how things get done at work. Overwhelmingly 90 percent of people in their study learn how to read the air (what this study refers to as *the unwritten rules*) by observing others and becoming aware of what behaviors are successful or unsuccessful.

In many workplaces, leaders and employees still engage in outdated behaviors that no longer serve them. So simply observing other people's behavior (consciously or not) and mimicking it is unlikely to help you develop your ability to navigate the new world of work. Instead, you need to become a conscious observer, which includes watching how people navigate the four informal systems and deciding if these behaviors will help you succeed.

To learn through observing, first identify examples of how people practice the new ideal worker behaviors as they relate to the four informal processes by reflecting on what they did. For example, consider how people build informal networks, share information, or access advancement opportunities. Reflecting on how other people behave significantly enhances your ability to learn. When we observe how people successfully build informal networks, share informal information, or access informal development and advancement opportunities, we can also use these behaviors to benchmark our ability.

Second, evaluate these behaviors to decide if engaging in them might be helpful for you—when it comes to the four informal processes. The goal is to continuously observe what ideal worker behaviors are practiced in your workplace. Only then can you identify what behaviors you want to engage in and practice them until they become a fundamental way of working.

Practice 2: Understanding: Learning from Your Peers

For the past three years, I have built my consultancy business, which specializes in helping businesses build healthy, inclusive cultures from the ground up. The business secured hundreds of clients worldwide with a healthy seven-figure turnover in just three years. My business is successful because I don't run it alone. I share the CEO position with Selina Suresh. We lead the business together because neither of us has run a business before. By doing it together, we learn from each other. Selina is my teacher; she provides me with constant advice, feedback, and guidance. And I do the same for her.

When it comes to informal learning, most people learn from *others*. Research has found that the primary way participants learn new skills on the job is by seeking out people who can share their informal learning experiences, model positive behaviors, and provide guidance and advice. *So, when it comes to informal learning, consider your coworkers your teachers, because they can help you understand whether your behaviors are effective or not.*

Selina lets me know if I need to adapt my behavior in team meetings, rework a proposal, or adjust my approach to managing specific clients. The Catalyst study found that 73 percent of people learn to read the air by regularly seeking feedback. Like Selina, your peers can help you learn by sharing their experiences, helping you solve real-life problems, and giving you feedback, advice, and support.

Ideally, you can identify two or three individuals who work closely with you—such as a peer, direct report, or line leader—who may be willing to share their perspectives, ideas, and observations. Discovering how to read the air is a social process because we learn what ideal worker behaviors are effective or not by the verbal and nonverbal feedback we receive from others.

While *most* of our informal learning happens through the interactions and feedback we receive from our direct supervisors and coworkers, hybrid working has made it more challenging to obtain informal feedback. In a virtual environment, you have fewer opportunities to observe your peers' nonverbal reactions, ask them questions, and seek advice or input on a project. These moments are often small and spontaneous, like when you pass a colleague in the hall or pop into your boss's office to ask them for advice. In a virtual setting, we must be far more deliberate about collating feedback by writing an email or bringing up a topic in a follow-up virtual one-to-one. Additionally, as I outlined in chapter two, hybrid working increases isolation. As people may be less connected to their peers, it is much harder for them to reach out and ask for feedback, or at least do it in real time as an issue arises.

For example, Selina and I have checkpoints in the week where we will have a Zoom call for fifteen to twenty minutes to review how things are going. If one of us provides feedback to the other person, we make sure it is as specific as possible, and we work together to identify what we want to change and how we can do that as part of our jobs. The other day, Selina noticed I couldn't answer some of a client's questions in a meeting. Straight after the meeting, Selina called me to check in and provide feedback. The conversation quickly moved to what we could do to prepare for meetings and prevent this from happening again in the future.

I frequently ask Selina for feedback and consistently provide her with feedback. Providing feedback has become second nature because we do it all the time. And, importantly, we don't make it weird. We don't build a formal document for people to fill in or make a big production out of asking for input. Instead, we continuously share feedback in real time and support each other to identify how to act on the feedback.

I created a model for how to give and receive feedback that anyone can use—the A-C-M model, illustrated below.

When giving someone feedback, start with the letter A, which stands for Awareness. You should assume good intent and help the person become aware of the impact their behavior is having. Once, when giving me feedback, Selina said, "Michelle, are you aware that in some of our client meetings, you don't seem as engaged as you normally do? You also struggle to answer some of our clients' questions, making them feel like we are not on top of everything." The goal is to help the other person understand the impact their behavior has so they can manage it. Awareness isn't enough, though; the next step is to help the other person understand what they can do differently. C stands for Corrective Action, and it includes detailing what behavior needs to change, and how. Selina went on to say, "Michelle, I think in the future we need to have a call ahead of our client meetings, and I can help you prepare for them if you have too much going on." Meaningful feedback should result in behavioral change. And finally there is M, which stands for Moving On. This is the hardest step. Receiving feedback can be difficult, but we make it harder when we get defensive, try to justify our behavior, center our feelings, or blame the other person. To prevent all of this, we need to move on.

To do this, the person receiving the feedback must also respond using three steps, which follow the same A-C-M acronym. Now A stands for Apologizing, which includes recognizing the impact your behavior is having and taking responsibility for it, while C and M retain their original definitions—Correcting Behavior and Moving On. In my exchange with Selina, I replied, "I am sorry that I am unprepared and disengaged in some of our client meetings. I have a lot going on and could really use help preparing for these, so thank you for your offer to support me. I will schedule the calls we need to prepare for client meetings and be clear on what I need your help with." When we apologize but don't share how we intend to change our behavior, the apology loses meaning. The A-C-M model is how we make giving and receiving informal feedback second nature.

The A-C-M Model of Feedback

GIVING FEEDBACK		RECEIVING FEEDBACK
Awareness of the impact	A	Apologize
Corrective action	C	Corrective action
Move on	M	Move on

The more you ask peers for informal feedback, the more comfortable you will get with initiating these conversations. The key is treating informal feedback like a data-gathering exercise. After all, it's just a practice of gathering informal information that will help you understand how to be more effective. Informal feedback also helps us understand how we need to respond to changes in our work environment and what skills we might need to learn as our workplaces change.

When I gather informal feedback, I write it down and then consider if there are similarities in what people say. Then I review their suggestions for what I could do differently, and even if I don't agree with some of the comments, the exercise helps me to identify how to apply the feedback provided. Feedback is only valuable if we know how to apply it.

Practice 3: Application: Learning Through Trial and Error

As part of my consulting business, I facilitate leadership development programs. I have facilitated numerous workshops in various companies and countries throughout my professional career. I didn't develop my facilitation skills overnight. The first time I facilitated, I was terrible. I learned all the technical presentation skills, like memorizing the speaker notes, preparing my PowerPoint slides, and practicing how I would speak. But to be a great facilitator, you need to know how to read the audience and respond to their feedback—in real time. Are they losing interest? Is the audience looking confused? Are their eyes glazing over because your delivery lacks energy, or are they having a food coma after lunch?

I learned how to facilitate by observing other facilitators in action and reflecting on what worked and didn't, so I had a clear idea of what good looked like. For instance, audiences tend not to laugh at speakers who try to be funny or tell a joke. Rather audience members tend to laugh when a person is just being themselves. So I generally avoid trying to tell an off-the-shelf joke.

To learn how to facilitate, I would also ask participants to share their takeaways to see what they recalled and what messages resonated. This would tell me what content wasn't resonating so I can improve how I deliver it next time. For example, I noticed that participants tend to remember story-related facts. So I always include a story when I want people to remember important content. I have been a facilitator for over twenty years and still follow the same process of observing what *good* looks like, reflecting on feedback, and applying what I learn.

Gathering and understanding informal feedback is one thing, but using it is quite another. I apply informal feedback because I want to manage the impact my behavior has on other people. The goal isn't just to be yourself at work *regardless of the impact*. If this were true, then you could say or do anything without caring how it makes other people feel. Instead, the aim is to understand how you can be your best self or, in my example, the best facilitator. Responding to informal feedback means recognizing that your behaviors may negatively impact your coworkers—and you—and then doing something about it.

We learn what works and what doesn't through trial and error, which includes experimenting with a new approach to see if it works or has a positive impact—much like how I learned the skill of facilitation. Experience comes from the practice of doing something repeatedly until it feels like second nature. For example, in the 2010 Catalyst study, 88 percent of participants learned how to read the air through trial and error. As you try out different behaviors, you determine what is working by observing your coworkers' reactions and asking for feedback. The goal is to identify the impact of your behavior because this is your reference point for understanding what worked and what did not.

We refine our ability to practice reading the air by continuously observing, seeking feedback, and then trialing new ways of working.

Move Your Mind

I recently read an old Zen parable where two men argue about a flag flapping in the wind.

"It's the wind that is moving the flag," says the first man.

"No, it's not! It's the flag that is really moving," says the second.

As the debate continues, a Zen master walks by and overhears the argument. Interrupting them both, he says, "Neither the flag nor the wind is moving. It is the mind that moves."

Your work environment will inevitably be a continuous source of change, but how you think about your potential will determine what you learn and how you develop throughout your career.

In the 2016 book *Mindset*, psychologist Carol Dweck argues that people think about their capabilities in two ways. Either people adopt a fixed mindset where they believe their talents and capabilities are set and cannot improve or they adopt a growth mindset, as they believe their skills, capabilities, and talent develop over time; they believe they can master a new skill with enough effort and persistence. How you think about learning determines what you learn.

If you have a fixed mindset and want to learn how to read the air, your first job is to shift your beliefs about your potential—your ability to learn new skills. For example, Shaun had a growth mindset because he was willing to learn a new way of leading and working. Likewise, each of us needs to cultivate a growth mindset to learn how to read the air. A 2015 academic research paper titled *What Are Drivers for Informal Learning?* found that 95 percent of people seeking out opportunities to learn informally do so because they are committed to their development. They want to learn new things, broaden their knowledge, and acquire new competencies to advance at work. With enough effort and consistency, anyone can develop their ability to read the air. This requires treating every project, task, or activity at work as an opportunity to refine how you work. Approaching your informal learning in this way (using the practices outlined in this chapter) is how you take ownership of your development.

Of course, the ideal worker behaviors associated with informal networks, information sharing, informal development, and advancement may vary in every work context. And they may even change, as workplaces do, which is why we need to change how we think about learning. Your ability to continuously learn is an outcome of being critically aware of changes to your work environment and responding to them. Learning to read the air isn't a one-off exercise. It's a habit we cultivate through awareness, understanding, and application.

6

INFORMAL ADVANCEMENT
How to Manage Your Career

"It's all been for nothing," Maya said as her eyes welled up with tears.

Maya was the chief people officer for a large multinational company in the United States and had been my supervisor for five years, but today was her last day at work. After twenty-five years of working for the same company, Maya decided to retire. At our celebratory lunch, I was expecting we'd discuss her plans for retired life. But instead, amid the buzz of the lunchtime crowd, I found myself trying to console a tearful Maya.

"I pursued position after position until I finally got the role I wanted," Maya said, wiping her tears with the back of her hand. "Now it's over, and it feels like it was all for nothing. Do you know what I mean?"

I nodded, even though I didn't really understand why she was so upset or how she could consider her life's work "nothing."

Unprompted, Maya continued, "I guess I just thought the title and the money would be enough. But it isn't. I feel empty. There must be more to work and life than this. Don't you think?"

I nodded. While I didn't understand all of what Maya felt, I did know that no one should feel like this at the end of their career.

The rhetorical question Maya asked me—*There must be more . . . don't you think?*—has haunted me for most of my career because I didn't know the answer.

Working in human resources for nearly twenty years, I have watched numerous leaders work countless hours, sacrificing time with their family and friends to get the next promotion. But their success was often short-lived. Companies would invariably encounter downsizing, recessions, and global competition, inevitably leading to restructures and layoffs. Leaders who'd fought so hard for a top spot would quickly be replaced. Unfortunately, many leaders who kept their jobs often did so by engaging in workplace politics, backstabbing, and infighting—and displaying the behaviors of the outdated "ideal worker."

Most of us, like Maya, have been encouraged to think of our careers as a series of predictable moves up a career ladder. Career success is about your ability to advance from one position to the next. So many people I worked with were so focused on arriving at the next promotion, position, and pay grade that they assumed, like Maya, that these achievements would be fulfilling. When Maya got promoted into the chief people officer role, she told me how happy she was for "finally making it!" *But career success isn't about arriving at a particular destination; instead, it's about what you leave behind.*

The root word for *success* comes from the Latin *exitus*, which means to exit. Career success is the contribution we make—everything we leave behind. Making a contribution is knowing what you did (whether completing a task, project, or role) and how you did it (by reading the air) positively impacted your teammates and your organization. Maya didn't know what her contribution was because she didn't know if people were better off for having worked with her. *Success isn't about arriving; it's about leaving your workplace better than you found it.*

While none of us can predict the future, we know that careers today are subject to increasing job insecurity, uncertainty, and ambiguity.

To navigate these challenges, we must proactively manage our careers by identifying our needs, learning how to meet them, and knowing how to find meaning in how we work regardless of what we do or where we do it. A 2022 study published in the *Review of Managerial Science* found that 30 percent of employees' perceptions of career success are directly attributable to their behaviors. This includes knowing how to adapt to new work demands, managing ambiguity, working with different groups of people, managing our feelings, and supporting coworkers with their mental and emotional health. These behaviors result from our ability to read ourselves, our coworkers, and our workplace. When we can read the air, we know how to manage our career advancement and fulfillment at work and, importantly, how to do this in a way that benefits everyone.

A New Career Path, a New Definition of Success

In the 1950s and 1960s, most people followed a traditional career path within a hierarchical organization. Employees would join a company, often for life, and progress up the career ladder, to achieve greater titles and pay. Employees valued stability and certainty from their employers. But fast-forward to today, when workplaces are becoming increasingly less hierarchical. With restructuring, layoffs, technological advancements, and recessions abounding, a job for life is not an option today. Careers change so much that they are often described as *protean*, a word derived from the ancient Greek word *proteus*, which means being capable of changing shape or form. To manage a protean career, you need to be flexible and adaptable in your approach and understand how careers have changed.

Through my research, I have summarized the most common significant career changes into four categories: self-managed, lifelong learning, boundaryless, and new measures of success.

Self-Managed

Careers today are self-managed. As employees, we get to decide on the career paths we want to pursue. We are no longer tied to one workplace or domain, so we can choose the company, role, or experience we want rather than waiting on one workplace to eventually provide the opportunity and settle for something else if it never does. There is no job for life; therefore, most of us will have to work for various organizations over our career lifetime. Consequently, most of us must ensure we have the skills needed to remain employed.

Lifelong Learning

The second major change is that most careers require *lifelong learning*. Gone are the days when one professional qualification or degree was enough to sustain you throughout your career. Most of us will have to adapt to changes in our work environment by learning new skills or acquiring new knowledge. Job security isn't something we can rely on our workplaces for. Instead, we create our job security by continuously learning and developing new skills so that we can continually find new jobs. There isn't a career ladder or hierarchy. Rather, careers have peaks and valleys because you might learn a new skill and specialize in one area, which is highly valued, and then these skills might become redundant as technology advances or jobs change.

Boundaryless

Our ability to learn new skills also includes learning new ways of working. The third significant change to careers is that they are *boundaryless* because hybrid working has enabled employees to work from home, from the office, and across geographies. Being mobile and knowing how to work both in person and in virtual environments is critical to succeeding in a hybrid workplace. As outlined in the introduction, most of us will increasingly have to learn to work in cross-cultural, geographically dispersed virtual environments. Consequently, knowing how to bridge our differences with others will become increasingly critical.

New Measures of Success

In the old days, employees based their job choices solely on a salary, role title, or hierarchical level—what academics refer to as objective *career success*. But our definition of career success has changed as careers have transitioned from the traditional career ladder to the protean career. No longer is a linear career path or job for life considered a measure of success. *Our definition of career success has changed because our careers have.* Maya was crying at lunch because although she had the salary and job title, she didn't feel like she had achieved anything beyond this. What she once found measurable didn't measure up. And she isn't alone; we all want to feel like we have contributed.

Success today, for most employees, is subjective—it's a career where they can pursue their career ambitions, develop their professional identity, and make an impact. Today, career success is more about our contribution—what we leave behind. Research has shown that how employees feel about their career accomplishments is more important to employees' perceptions of career success than salary growth. So it isn't surprising that research has also shown that employees are more likely to make career decisions based on subjective criteria, like what motivates them and what they value—what is known as subjective career success. When it comes to protean careers, employees decide if their careers are a success based on the extent to which there is alignment between what they value (like psychological safety) and what their workplace offers (like feeling included). Career success today is more about undertaking work that aligns with your values.

When it comes to our careers, what we value influences what we need from our employers. In the past, we valued status and stability. Consequently, we needed workplaces that offered job stability and rigid career progression. In protean careers, research has shown, most people value freedom and growth. Specifically, we value the freedom to be ourselves, pursue opportunities to develop, realize our potential, and contribute. For example, I value learning and development, which means I need to work for an organization that will give me the freedom to try new ways of working and explore novel ideas. Your needs are more likely to be met if you work in an organization that values what you do.

Getting to Know Your Needs

While protean careers increase our need for freedom and growth, we may have additional needs we want our workplaces to fulfill. Knowing what our needs are is the first step to meeting them—so we don't end up like Maya, wondering if there must have been more to life than hustling for the next promotion or pay raise. Subjective career success is the degree to which our career needs are fulfilled, which is why it is essential to understand what you need from your workplace and how to meet these needs.

A 2009 academic study examined the needs employees have at work and identified a hierarchy of five needs all employees have.

All employees first need to feel *physically and psychologically safe* at work. We all need to know that we won't be physically harmed, discriminated against, harassed, or marginalized at work. This need is universal and the foundation for meeting all other needs. Suppose you don't feel physically and psychologically safe. In that case, it is impossible to feel like you belong or to make a meaningful contribution because all your mental, emotional, and physical energy is spent on keeping yourself safe.

If your need for physical and psychological safety isn't met, it's impossible to fulfill your second need, which is feeling like you *belong*. As I outlined in chapter two, we all want to feel connected and accepted by the people we work with. But belonging also requires that we feel represented in our workplaces—so that we don't feel alone. We all need to see other people who look like us reflected in the makeup of our workplaces because it's an obvious way of knowing your workplace values people like you. We belong when there is a match between what we value and what our workplace values.

If you don't feel like you belong, it is challenging to speak up, share your ideas, and collaborate with your teammates. Yet belonging is a prerequisite to fulfilling our desire to make a *meaningful contribution*—the third need. Most of us want to feel appreciated, recognized, and rewarded for our work. The more we feel appreciated for what we do, the more we want to take on and contribute.

As we take on more work and responsibility, we often have to learn new skills. As I shared in chapter five, the way we learn at work is often informal and self-directed. We need the *freedom to learn and develop* by pursuing what interests us—the fourth need. To meet this need, we have to take ownership of what we learn and how we learn it. Finally, we need our workplaces to support our development. This includes providing feedback and encouragement to try new ways of working—as we know from chapter four, this is the only way to truly master the universal skills most of us will need to succeed!

We want to be recognized for learning, developing, and mastering new skills. Our fulfillment at work comes from feeling *recognized as competent professionals*—the fifth need. In a protean career, your employability isn't limited to one organization—you no longer rely on one company for job security. Instead, your employability results from your ability to learn and grow. You feel fulfilled at work when you master a new skill and are recognized for that—because recognition is how we understand our impact. You understand the positive impact your behavior has on your teammates through the recognition they provide. Like when a teammate thanks you for how you managed a project or the advice you provided. The more your needs are met, the more successful you will feel because you have made a contribution beyond a job title or salary.

Why We Quit . . . Quietly

Imagine feeling like Maya did, but you still have another twenty years left until you retire. Then, likely, you would mentally and emotionally check out of your job. Unfortunately, doing so has become so commonplace that the term "quiet quitting" in 2022 trended on social media. Quiet quitting refers to the growing number of employees who remain with their employer but refuse to go above and beyond the tasks outlined in their job description. Instead, these employees have simply checked out as they do just enough to get a monthly paycheck but nothing more.

A 2022 article published in *Harvard Business Review* titled "Quiet Quitting Is About Bad Bosses, Not Bad Employees" stated that when it comes to quiet quitting, the most important factor is a breach of trust. As I outlined in chapter two, workplaces are one giant trust exchange. Employees give their time, effort, and knowledge, assuming that the organization will reciprocate by giving them pay and time off (objective measures of success) and opportunities to learn and develop (subjective measures of success). Most workplaces meet employees' objective measures of success because they have to—such measures as pay and leave are often stipulated in a contract. But many workplaces are not meeting employees' subjective measures of success, which breaks trust.

The *Harvard Business Review* article finds that employees quietly quit when their leaders solely focus on assigning tasks and expecting results (the *what* of work). These leaders don't manage *how* the work gets done by offering a supportive environment and demonstrating concern for their teammates. Employees are four times more likely to quit when their manager focuses on results at the expense of meeting their employees' needs. Additionally, a 2022 study published in the *Review of Managerial Science* found that when managers don't meet employees' needs, the employees don't believe they will succeed, and their well-being tends to suffer. The bottom line is you are less likely to succeed when your workplace does not meet your needs.

When your needs are met, your workplace benefits because you are much more likely to be engaged, innovate, problem-solve, collaborate, and contribute in a meaningful way. In the *Review of Managerial Science* study, managers who supported employees to fulfill their needs saw 62 percent in extra effort on the job—like putting in extra hours and taking on additional tasks. The more your needs are met, the more likely you are to succeed. For example, if you value learning and development, you need to consider how your workplace will fulfill your need to learn and grow. Likewise, suppose you feel your coworkers devalue your difference. In that case, you know your workplace isn't meeting a basic need for psychological safety, making it very difficult for you to succeed. The more employees contribute, the more likely they are to be objectively and subjectively successful.

Today many employees—like Maya—work for organizations that do not meet one or more of their needs, which is why they are unhappy. It is difficult to measure the exact number of employees who quietly quit in 2022 because these employees remain employed. However, *The State of the Global Workplace 2022 Report* by Gallup found that most employees don't find their work meaningful, as only 21 percent of employees reported being engaged in their work. In addition, only 33 percent said they are thriving in their overall mental and emotional well-being. Participants in this study described their experiences of working life as "living for the weekend" and "watching the clock." Many employees are treating their jobs as a means to an end, which means by the new standard of career success, they are not succeeding. To succeed, we need to manage our careers, including knowing how to meet our needs even when our workplaces don't.

Your Number One Job

Maya managed her career by simply waiting for her company to offer the next role or promotion. Her workplace was in charge of her advancement. When Maya's boss left the company, she finally got promoted. The only action Maya took to manage her career was making her ambitions known to her boss and then waiting it out. Protean careers transfer responsibility for career management from workplaces to employees. That means you have to proactively manage your career because no one else will. Career advancement doesn't happen by chance; instead, it happens through the actions we consistently take to manage our careers, but the problem is most of us do not know what these actions are. A 2021 study published in the *Review of Managerial Science* found that career-planning behaviors—like setting goals and objectives for your career—are generally not commonly practiced. While this study didn't explain why we don't manage our careers, I suspect many of us don't know how or are still relying on our workplaces to direct our career paths.

Based on my review of the research, it's clear that managing careers generally includes three things: *know why, know who,* and *know how.* In the academic literature, knowing your why for work refers to the extent to which you know your needs, abilities, interests, values, aspirations, and work preferences. It is the ability to know what you value and need. Managing your career starts with being aware of your needs, strengths, and capabilities. Maya was considered by many of her teammates to be successful. But I know Maya feels like she failed because she didn't manage her career. Maya never knew what she needed—like the need to make a meaningful contribution.

A 2022 academic study in the *Journal of Vocational Behavior* found that the nature of protean careers requires that individuals take responsibility for managing their career path. To manage your career is to know what your needs are so you can meet them.

Knowing who can support you is about being able to develop a wide range of relationships with people who can provide informal information, guidance, advice, and support, as well as advocate for your career advancement. Essentially when we know who can support us at work, we know how to meet our needs. This study also found that individuals who are clear about what they value and need from their organizations (like their career priorities and learning requirements) and take responsibility for meeting their needs and managing their careers report higher levels of subjective career success. Your career advancement depends on your ability to manage your informal relationships to access opportunities for career development and advancement, which requires the ability to read the air.

Knowing how to develop and grow is critical, given that workplaces are continuously changing. While traditional career paths encouraged people to develop specialized knowledge and skills, the protean boundaryless career requires the ability to develop transferable skills. Managing your career is a never-ending exercise that requires the ability to read the air so you can know how workplaces are changing and what skills you need to develop to remain employable.

In the following section, I will outline the specific practices you can use to manage your career—uncovering your *why*, your *who*, and your *how*. However, while we all need to take action to manage our careers, the process will look a little different for each of us. Your upbringing, socioeconomic status, education, physical or mental abilities, personality traits, and demographic characteristics all have a significant role to play in supporting or hindering your career success. As I shared in my first book, *The Fix*, careers don't unfold in the same way for everyone because workplaces often devalue individual differences. Therefore, people from typically underrepresented groups have to overcome challenges due to discrimination and harassment that those in dominant groups do not.

Acknowledging inequality is important when it comes to career management because leaders need to remove the obstacles to career advancement that they create. A 2010 academic research study published in *Industrial Relations* found career satisfaction is typically lower for racial and ethnic minority employees because of the discrimination and marginalization they experience. This research also found when it comes to employee career satisfaction, the most important factor is the support and recognition employees receive from their managers. Unfortunately, leaders are not taking action to remove the marginalization, discrimination, and inequity (they often create) in hiring, developing, rewarding, helping, and promoting employees. A research study by Catalyst found a manager's inclusive leadership behaviors explain roughly 45 percent of employees' experiences of inclusion. The more excluded and dissatisfied you feel at work, the less likely you are to stay. Leaders who do not take action to build inclusive teams simply won't be able to harness the diverse talents and capabilities their employees have to innovate, problem-solve, and create. In the long run, businesses that cannot retain and include a diverse workforce won't be able to outcompete their competitors.

While this might be comforting for anyone experiencing discrimination at work to know, it can also feel deflating. Many of us don't want to wait for our workplaces to become more equitable and inclusive. The good news is that protean careers shift responsibility for career management from your workplace to *you*. That means the more you take action to manage your career, the more satisfied you are likely to feel when it comes to work and life in general. But if you don't manage your career, it can lead to feelings of helplessness—like going through the motions of completing a job you hate because it pays the bills or hoping someone will eventually retire so you can take their spot.

Career management isn't simply jumping from one workplace to the next, hoping to find an inclusive organization. Besides, most of us cannot just quit our jobs; we have bills to pay—that's why so many people opt for *quietly quitting*. Instead, career management is knowing what you need and taking action to fulfill these needs. There is a ton of academic research examining protean careers and how people can advance, most of which supports the idea that people who take action to manage their careers have the highest levels of employability. When you take action to manage your career, you can gain and maintain employment because you have the skills and capabilities workplaces need. In addition, the more employable you are, the more you get to decide what organizations you want to work for. People who wait on their company to manage their careers have the lowest levels of employability, which also reduces their career satisfaction. Everyone deserves to have a fulfilling career, but this starts with each of us recognizing and valuing our needs so that we can take responsibility and action to fulfill them.

Knowing Why, Who, and How: The Three Practices of Career Management

Maya didn't know if she was successful or not because she had never defined what career success meant to her. Disappointed, empty, and lost on the last day of work are feelings nobody wants to have. The only way to guarantee this won't be your experience is to take ownership of your experience of work.

Our careers are a combination of experiences we have in working life and the meaning we give to those experiences. A meaningful career is an outcome of three things. First, you need to know what gives you meaning at work—referred to in academia as *know why*. Second, you need to know how to build meaningful relationships at work—*know who*. Third, you need to know what impact you make at work—*know how*. Together, these three elements—*know what, know why*, and *know how*—give our work experiences meaning. When we feel like we are making a contribution and enjoy the people we work with—and the work we undertake—we are more likely to feel fulfilled.

Many journal articles refer to these three elements in different ways, but most articles agree that these are the competencies you need to manage your career today. Research has found that all three career competencies play a significant role in our subjective career success and employability. These three career competencies are essential for everyone, regardless of the different career aspirations people might have. While you might think that protean careers are better suited to people who enjoy change and uncertainty, research has shown career satisfaction isn't a result of personality differences. Rather, career satisfaction depends on the proactive behaviors people engage in to manage their careers. Career success is an outcome of the actions we take to manage our experience of work.

Practice 1: Know Your Why for Work

I was recently in Tokyo visiting my Japanese friend Mei. We met in a small tearoom, which served the most delicious delicate handmade cakes and pastries, for Sencha, a loose-leaf green tea. Tucked away in a back corner of the tearoom, Mei quizzed me about my research. I began explaining the three career competencies and was halfway through sharing what *know why* meant when Mei's eyes lit up, and she exclaimed, "Ahh, you mean *ikigai*!" Confused, I shook my head. Then, Mei explained, "*Ikigai* is having a sense of meaning in life, being motivated to pursue your passion, and feeling fulfilled."

Mei is right: *ikigai* is a great way to think about your know why. In Japanese culture, *ikigai* encompasses all elements of life—including a person's career, hobbies, relationships, and spirituality. It usually means the feelings of accomplishment and fulfillment that follow when you pursue your passion. From a work perspective, *ikigai* is the contribution we make—it's everything we leave behind.

Most of us will spend an average of forty to fifty years of our lives at work, so it is imperative to invest time and energy in understanding what will create a sense of *ikigai*. A 2008 research study titled *Sense of Life Worth Living (Ikigai) and Mortality in Japan: Ohsaki Study*, which included more than forty-three thousand Japanese adults, found that mortality risk is significantly higher for people who do not find a sense of *ikigai*. The main reason for this is that people who have found *ikigai* enjoy their work; they want to live longer so they can pursue what gives them a sense of meaning. Ikigai *is life-affirming; it's what makes work worth doing.*

Importantly, from a work perspective, *ikigai* isn't just what you might hope to achieve; it's awareness of the contribution you want to make—that is what you want to leave behind. When you know your *ikigai*, you understand why you do what you do.

Many researchers and authors recommend asking yourself questions to reflect on what gives you meaning in life—What do you love? Or what is your passion? What are you good at? What does the world need? But these questions are not work-related and are so broad they could apply to anything.

To define your why for work, you want to be able to write down a why statement, which is a sentence or two that clearly outlines why you do what you do. For example, when I write a new book or start a new research project, which is my work, I always write down my why statement and stick it up on my wall because it reminds me to spend my time and energy at work focused on what gives me meaning.

You can write a why statement for any task, job, goal, or activity you want to undertake. For example, before writing this book, I took some time to define my why statement: *I want to write a book that changes how we work together so that every person feels seen, heard, and valued for who they are and what they contribute.* Regarding this book, success is not how many copies I sell. Instead, success is the extent to which I believe (subjectively) that I fulfilled my why—whether I feel like I wrote a book that will help people feel valued for who they are and what they contribute at work. My why motivates and sustains me throughout the process of writing a book.

As an executive coach, one of the techniques I use to help clients identify their why statements is to play back their responses by asking them why and having them answer. You can use this technique to identify your why. All you need is one person to ask the questions and one person to respond. The process includes the following steps:

First, identify something you want to do, achieve, or aspire to. For example, I wanted to write this book.

Second, get someone to ask why you want to achieve this objective and keep your answer to one sentence. For example, I wanted to write a book to share my research and work over the last two decades.

Third, get someone to play back the response by reframing the answer as a why question. Again, try to keep your answer to one sentence. For example, someone might ask me: "Why do you want to share your research and work?"

And my response would be: "I want people to understand how workplaces work."

Fourth, get someone to play back the response again by reframing the answer as a why question. Again, try to keep your answer to one sentence. For example, someone might ask me: "Why do you want to write a book that helps people understand how workplaces work?"

And my response would be: "I want people to know how to work better together."

Fifth, get someone to play back the response again by reframing the answer as a why question. Try to keep your answer to one sentence. For example, someone might ask me: "Why do you want people to know how to work better together?"

And my response would be: "I believe every person deserves to feel seen, heard, and valued for who they are and what they contribute at work."

The person asking the questions needs to make sure they provide you with enough time to reflect and respond to each question. The person asking the questions mustn't judge or criticize the responses. Their job is to ask the questions and write down the responses.

Generally, by the fourth or fifth time someone has played back your response by asking why, you will have nothing new to add. So, when you are at this point, you can stop and take all the responses and combine them into a why statement. That is how I wrote my why statement for this book.

Why statements are powerful because they encapsulate all you hope to achieve and leave behind. Out of the three career competencies, research has shown, knowing your why is most important when it comes to subjective career success. This finding makes sense, given that the meaning and satisfaction we derive from work results from knowing our why.

Thanks to the boundaryless protean career, you don't have to stay in one job, which means our careers have become a path to self-discovery. Most of us will have different whys for different things, and our whys might change throughout our careers. Research finds when you know your why your identity isn't tied to one workplace or job. Your why guides your sense of self. When you know your why, you are also more willing and motivated to try new things, learn new skills, and adapt to changes in your workplace. We can learn new skills, explore different occupations, and identify what work we enjoy doing—if we take the time to identify why we are doing it.

Practice 2: Know Who Can Advocate for Your Career

Once a month, generally on a Friday night, Mark, a junior account executive I coach, will meet up with Barry, a senior leader in his company, at the local pub for a beer. Barry and Mark are friendly but wouldn't describe each other as close friends. Barry provides Mark with advice, support, and guidance that help Mark succeed at work. Mark shares his challenges with Barry, who listens, asks questions, and brainstorms solutions. At drinks, Barry will often share inside information that Mark might benefit from knowing, like upcoming organizational changes and potential career opportunities. Both Mark and Barry get a lot out of their relationship. Mark gets invaluable career advice and support, and Barry feels he is making a meaningful contribution to his organization by supporting a future leader. Of course, Mark and Barry believe they are just meeting up for a beer. But in reality, Barry and Mark are engaging in informal mentoring.

The term *mentor* dates back to Greek mythology and describes the relationship between an older experienced adult and a younger protégé, typically male. The older male will help the younger male build his self-esteem and identity throughout the mentoring relationship. More recently, the term *sponsor* has been used to reference leaders who go beyond mentoring and provide their protégé with access to their network and use their influence to help the protégé advance. Most mentoring or sponsorship relationships are built on a solid foundation of trust because these relationships are informal.

Research examining why men advance at work at higher rates than women has pointed to mentoring or sponsorship as the reason. The belief is that women are not mentored as much as men, but this isn't true. A 2018 *Harvard Business Review* article titled "Women Ask for Raises as Often as Men but Are Less Likely to Get Them" cited research examining forty-six hundred employees across eight hundred organizations that found that men and women do not differ in their reported levels of mentoring. Women are mentored as much as men, and in some cases, more, but the type of mentoring men and women receive is different.

Men, like Mark, are more likely to have mentoring relationships with senior executives who provide inside information about how the organization works and are willing to use their influence to help their mentees advance. We like people who are similar to us and want to support them to be successful. It's what gives work meaning. This is why men are much more likely to informally mentor or sponsor other men than women.

To overcome the exclusionary nature of informal mentoring, companies will often implement a formal mentoring program whereby a senior leader is paired with a more junior employee and asked to mentor them for some time. The challenge with this is that mentoring is a relationship based on trust. When we formalize mentoring, we make it weird. We force people together; as a result, the interactions are often stilted and awkward. Over time the relationship feels like an obligation, which erodes trust. Informal mentoring happens organically, as people seek each other out for friendship, advice, guidance, and support. Despite companies investing in formal mentoring programs, research by Yale University professor Marissa D. King has found that 82 percent of women and 84 percent of men find their work mentors informally. The value of mentoring comes from relationships that develop informally.

The problem with informal mentoring and sponsorship is that it's exclusionary. Research finds that very few white male protégés have mentors of another gender. Instead, senior leaders select employees they like, who often are a lot like them, to mentor. Mentoring and sponsorship work in the traditional career path, where all you need to get the next promotion is one person, like Barry, who is willing to take you under their wing. According to a 2019 research study published in *Harvard Business Review*, 75 percent of professional men and women want to have a mentor, but only 37 percent have one.

In a protean career, you cannot rely on one person to support your advancement or even two because you are likely to change your career path or employer several times. You need to develop a range of connections with people who can advocate for your career—both within and outside your workplace. The responsibility for managing your career lies with you. We can't depend on our workplaces to offer us the support or mentoring we need. Instead, we must proactively seek out and cultivate relationships with people who can advocate for our career advancement.

In the old world of work, mentoring and sponsorship were informal systems leaders would use to support, advance, and promote people who looked like them. But as I shared in chapter two, companies can no longer afford to advance one type of leader to succeed. Organizations need to harness diverse talent to innovate, problem-solve, create, and ultimately outcompete their competitors. In the new world of work, mentors and sponsors are not as critical as career advocates. A career advocate is a person who understands your why for work and is willing to champion you to fulfill it. The career advocate is usually someone willing to provide advice, support, coaching, inside information, connections with helpful people, opportunities to engage in meaningful work, or use their position to advocate for your advancement by putting your name forward or recommending you for opportunities.

Research has found that career advocates increase a person's access to high-profile projects, promotion opportunities, pay, and overall career satisfaction. Importantly, a career advocate levels the playing field for everyone. Numerous studies between 2001 and 2010, cited in the white paper *Advocacy vs. Mentoring* by Sylvia Ann Hewlett Associates, have demonstrated how advocacy amplifies the careers of people from typically underrepresented groups at work.

Once you know your why for work, you can start identifying potential career advocates who can help you realize your goal; ideally, you want at least two career advocates (or people who could become an advocate) within and two outside your organization. Relying on one career advocate is risky, as that person could leave the organization at any time. Importantly, you will know if you have a career advocate versus a mentor or sponsor because this person usually acts as a career advocate to a diverse group of people, regardless of their identity. Career advocates are also willing to connect you with people inside and outside the organization. Mentors and sponsors tend to rely on internal connections, limiting the diversity of the connections they can offer you.

Identifying someone who could advocate for your career is one thing but establishing a relationship with them will take time and effort. Specifically, establishing a career advocate is similar to most relationships; you must invest in building a strong connection. A 2016 academic research study published in the *Social Science Journal* found there are certain behaviors people engage in to build strong connections. These include being candid, sharing personal information, having mutual interests, demonstrating care and concern, and sharing similar values. If you want to build a strong connection with a career advocate, it is vital to spend time getting to know the person so you can understand if they share your values and interests. Then, as you build your relationship, you can be honest and open about your career aspirations and invite them to share theirs.

The strength of the connection you form with a career advocate determines the investment they are willing to make to help you realize your why for work. As I outlined in chapter four, reciprocity is the key to successful relationships, especially at work. Taking time to understand your career advocates' goals and aspirations will help you identify ways you can support their development and demonstrate care and concern for their advancement. Research finds when you support another person's advancement, it benefits you because advocating for someone else's career increases your job satisfaction and commitment. It also broadens your network, increases access to information, and even enhances your reputation (especially when the person you are advocating for succeeds). That is why it is essential to seek career advocates and try to be one yourself.

Practice 3: Know-How to Manage Your Reputation

One of the main reasons Maya wasn't subjectively successful in her career is that she didn't know herself beyond a title. Her identity at work was tied to her position and pay, which were only temporary. Maya is so much more than her position and title—only she doesn't know it, which is why she felt so empty at lunch. Maya is a caring, kind, supportive, and inclusive leader. She loved working with people and knew how to build a culture where most people felt valued, which is why her company had high retention rates, employee satisfaction, and engagement scores. What gives Maya meaning in her work is supporting, developing, and coaching others to succeed. Had Maya known this earlier in her career, she would have sought out more opportunities to fulfill these needs and engage in work that she found meaningful.

It's not enough to continuously develop new skills. Know-how is about understanding how to manage the value other people assign to your skills. In other words, know-how is the ability to manage your reputation to maintain your employability. Your reputation is created and maintained by other people's perceptions of how you work and the contribution you make. It's what you are known for and what you leave behind.

As most of us will have multiple career paths with multiple organizations, our employability depends on how well we can manage our reputations. Career success is much more subjective in protean careers because we determine if we are successful by how other people perceive the contribution we make. Humans are social animals who want people to see them as they see themselves. Therefore, you manage your reputation by understanding how other people perceive you and the contribution you make.

To manage your career, knowing how to manage your reputation is essential. Research has found that employees at all levels of the organization are more likely to be hired and promoted if they maintain a positive reputation. A CEO's reputation (good or bad) is so essential to a business's success it can even affect stock prices (positively or negatively). Unfortunately, we often confuse managing our reputation with self-promotion and showing off. However, research has also shown that your reputation results from the assessments people make about your *actions* and the *intention* behind those actions. To know your reputation, you must learn how to read the air to understand how other people perceive you. Chapter four outlines specific practices you can use to build your self-awareness.

But knowing your reputation is one thing; managing it is something else. Typically, researchers studying how people build reputations assume that the most talented or capable people will have the best reputation, but this isn't so. On a team of high performers, everyone is good at *what they do*—in terms of the tasks they undertake. So, to build a positive reputation, we must manage *how we work*—when it comes to engaging and collaborating with others.

The 2017 academic study *Establishing a Reputation* found that the more a person deviates (positively or negatively) from group norms—which the researchers defined as the unwritten rules for how people interact, collaborate, and behave at work—the more their reputation suffers or is enhanced. The norm of reciprocity, outlined in chapter two, governs most of our interactions at work. Generally, people expect that you will behave with their best interests in mind; when you don't—you take credit for someone else's work or steal a colleague's idea—you become untrustworthy, and your reputation suffers. Conversely, your reputation is enhanced when you go above and beyond to support your coworkers—like ensuring people are publicly recognized for their project contributions. The key to building a positive reputation is predictability, which includes consistently behaving in a way that has the best interests of your coworkers in mind. When we deviate from how people expect us to behave, we become unpredictable, which makes us difficult to trust. Your reputation is the degree to which people can trust you.

Even if someone has one exceptional achievement—like a big sale—this doesn't mean their reputation will be positive. Instead it is how predictable their behavior is that builds or breaks trust. In my

PhD research, I discovered three practices people engage in to build trust at work. These are clarity, transparency, and consistency.

Clarity includes being clear about what you value and need from your workplace. For example, I began my career in London nearly fifteen years ago as a human resources manager. I worked for Jon, the country manager of our office in Syria. On Jon's first day, he held a meeting with his leadership team, which included me. Jon shared three values that mattered to him—teamwork, excellence, and communication. Jon explained what these values meant to him and why they were important. When you communicate what you need from your workplace, people understand your intentions and why you do what you do. Likewise, the clearer you are, the more people can predict how you are likely to behave, making you trustworthy.

To maintain this predictability, you must be transparent about why you do what you do. *Transparency* means openly sharing the reasons behind your behavior and decisions at work. For example, when Jon decided to promote a leader, he would share what they achieved and detailed examples of how they did this in a way that demonstrated teamwork, excellence, and communication. The more you can articulate and share why you do what you do, the more people understand who you are and what you value.

Consistency is the key to managing your reputation because reputations take time to establish. The more a person regularly behaves in a certain way, the more you can predict how likely it is that they will engage in this behavior in the future. At least once a month, Jon would ask two or three employees for feedback on how effectively he demonstrates teamwork, excellence, and communication. Jon used this feedback to identify how he could be more consistent in demonstrating what he valued in how he delivered his work. The more consistent you are, the more people rely on you to behave in a way that is aligned with what you value. Building a reputation requires consistency in behavior—behaving in a way aligned with what you value and need from your workplace.

To build your reputation, it is important to regularly reflect on how you can be more clear, transparent, and consistent. And if you don't know, ask your teammates for feedback and input on how you can improve. For example, you can ask people for feedback using these questions: When it comes to my behavior, do you know what to expect from me at work? What do you think I value at work—specifically regarding how I work? Do you understand why I behave the way I do or the reasoning behind my decisions? Or are you often surprised by my behavior? How could I be more open about the decisions I make? Do you find my behavior to be inconsistent? What can I do to better manage how I work, so you know what to expect from me?

Our ability to build a positive personal reputation is how we fill many of our needs at work, like the need to belong, make a meaningful contribution, and be recognized as competent professionals. Likewise, our needs motivate us to build a positive reputation. For example, our need to belong increases our motivation to engage in positive interactions and build strong relationships. The more you can be clear, consistent, and transparent in your behavior, the more you will be able to manage your reputation, enhancing your ability to contribute and derive meaning from your work.

Set Yourself Free

You may have heard the story of the elephant and the rope. It is a well-known story about a man passing a herd of elephants when he noticed they are all tied to a tree with a small thin rope.

"There are no chains! No cages!" he exclaimed.

Alarmed that the elephants could break free at any time, the man found their trainer and asked why the animals were not kept in a secure enclosure.

"Well, when they were younger and a lot smaller, we used the same rope to tie them up. It was enough to secure them. They are now conditioned to believe they cannot break away, so they don't even try. They don't even know they are free."

No one wants to feel how Maya did at the end of her career. To prevent this, we must take action to set ourselves free by managing our careers. The more you manage your career, the more employable you are. And the more employable you are, the more choice you have about who you work for and the more freedom you have to engage in work that you find worthwhile.

Like the elephant herd, we must take back our freedom by managing our careers rather than quietly quitting. When we quietly quit, we stay tied to jobs and careers that no longer serve us. When we don't know how to manage our careers, we feel helpless and trapped in a meaningless job—this is how we quit on ourselves. When you manage your career, you reclaim your freedom to choose the experiences and the meaning you want to gain from the time you spend at work.

Importantly, when you manage your career, it benefits others. At first, this fact might seem counterintuitive because protean careers involve you prioritizing your career aspirations ahead of your company's goals. But a 2018 research study published in the *Annual Review of Organizational Psychology and Organizational Behavior* found that protean careers make us better coworkers, which improves our organizations. This finding is called the *protean paradox*. This paradox exists because protean careers require you to manage your subjective career success, which includes engaging in work aligned with your values and fulfilling your career needs. When your needs are met, you are more likely to feel engaged in your work, committed to your workplace, and satisfied with your career. Had just one elephant tried to pull itself free from the rope, they might have freed the entire herd. Managing your career is how you manage your work experience and, ultimately, what you leave behind.

7

PAY IT FORWARD

How to Find Meaning at Work

Throughout this book, I have shared how learning to read the air is how we learn to connect with our workplace, our colleagues, and ourselves. We belong and find meaning at work by reading the air.

Often when leaders talk about finding meaning and purpose at work, they will share the well-known story of President John F. Kennedy visiting NASA for the first time in 1962. The story goes that President Kennedy toured NASA and met a janitor walking down the hallway. The president stopped the janitor and asked him what he did for NASA. The janitor replied, "I'm helping put a man on the moon."

Leaders love the idea that the person making the least amount of money and doing the most monotonous job can find meaning in their work if they connect what they do to the products or services the workplace offers. However, academic research, including my own, paints a very different picture.

Even when companies encourage employees to connect what they do to their organization's achievements, they miss the point. Simply chasing one achievement (like increasing a company's share price, profits, or productivity) to the next isn't what makes work meaningful. Meaningful work is the degree to which a person experiences their job as valuable and worthwhile beyond simply completing a task. So while some achievements—like putting a man on the moon for the first time—can feel tremendous, they don't sustain our sense of meaning at work.

How would the janitor respond to the president's question today?

"I am helping to put the thirteenth man on the moon" doesn't have the same ring. We are more than what we or our workplaces do.

Leaders want employees to find meaning in their work because studies show doing so increases employee engagement, productivity, and innovation. A 2020 study published in *Management Research Review* found that when employees don't feel a sense of meaning, their performance, effort, satisfaction, engagement, and motivation at work decrease. In turn, this significantly increases employee absenteeism and turnover. Employees quit or quietly quit because their work is not worth doing. The more companies try to tell employees to find meaning in what they do or produce, the less likely employees are to believe them and the more likely they are to quit.

Much research investigating how we find meaning at work has focused on the jobs people perform—the "putting a man on the moon approach." But increasingly, research has recognized the critical role relationships and communities at work play in building our sense of meaning. It could be argued that in the 1960s, it was important for employees—like the janitor—to feel a connection to what their workplace did because employees rarely changed careers or employers. Back then, workplaces were responsible for managing employees' careers, so it makes sense that employees would also look to their workplaces to give them a sense of meaning. As discussed in the last chapter, traditional careers focused almost exclusively on what was achieved rather than how it was achieved. Today, companies continue to encourage the idea that the more you achieve, the more meaningful your career is. Or that if you don't find your job meaningful, the company's success—and your contribution to it—should be enough to make up for the lack.

But for work to be truly meaningful to the modern employee, we need to identify our contribution beyond the tasks we perform or the results we achieve. Meaning isn't handed to us by our workplaces; it's something we discover in learning how we work together. Despite the common myth that our salary and wealth should predict our happiness, research has shown that the quality of our relationships in life and work does. A 2014 review of over 1,336 academic journal articles found that other people matter most when it comes to our happiness. *People derive a sense of meaning at work through their connections to others.*

Most of us want more meaning at work—and badly. A 2018 study by BetterUp surveyed 2,285 American professionals and found that nine out of ten employees, regardless of their job level, tasks, or salary, are willing to trade a percentage of their lifetime earnings for greater meaning at work. Moreover, participants were willing to forgo 23 percent of their total future earnings (almost as much as people spend on housing) to have a job that gave them meaning!

If employees found meaning in what they do or what their companies achieve, they wouldn't feel the need to quit quietly. Could there be anything more demoralizing than spending most of your waking hours working for a boss or with coworkers who don't appreciate, support, engage, encourage, or include you? If this is your work experience, you might wonder why you should give more than you need to. Work isn't your whole life, so why go above and beyond? Surely your health, happiness, and well-being are more important than a job. While all of these arguments for quiet quitting are valid, they miss one important fact: we are our workplaces.

Your organization isn't a place, room, or building. Instead, work-

places are a community—much like a forest—composed of people, including you, who are connected by their shared contribution.

How committed you are to your workplace is a direct result of the behaviors you engage in. In academia, organizational citizenship behavior is a term used to describe the voluntary positive behaviors employees engage in at work beyond their job description. Like when a colleague is swamped and struggling to complete their tasks, and you offer to help them, or you load paper into the communal printer or make suggestions for improving your workplace. A common term for this is *paying it forward*, which describes everything we voluntarily do that supports and benefits our coworkers and organization.

Organizational citizenship behaviors are not formally rewarded with increased pay or promotions, nor are they formally performed in the formal process and procedures of the company. People engage in these behaviors because they notice something, sense a need, or feel a connection and compassion for coworkers. They read the air and behave in a way that has the best interests of their colleagues in mind. Who doesn't appreciate a coworker offering to stay late to help them meet a deadline?

When employees pay it forward, research has found that it positively impacts both the individual and the organization. Engaging in organizational citizenship behaviors has increased employees' morale, performance, relationships, job satisfaction, mental and emotional well-being, and sense of belonging. When people voluntarily help others, it increases their overall life satisfaction, decreases depression, lowers blood pressure, and even increases longevity. Also, when employees engage in these behaviors, it increases customer satisfaction, employee collaboration, and the quality and quantity of work produced.

We are the communities *we* work in, which means we have the potential to create a meaningful experience by engaging in behaviors that support our community. A 2020 academic study published in the *Journal of Theoretical Social Psychology* found that we enhance our commitment to our workplaces when we engage in behaviors that support our coworkers—either remotely or in person. The more you pay it forward at work, the more meaning you derive from your work and the more committed you are likely to feel.

Aside from sleep, work is where we spend most of our waking hours over our lifetime. How we experience work is how we experience a considerable amount of our lives, which is why managing the meaning we derive from work is essential to our health, happiness, and general well-being.

Put Paying It Forward Into Practice

Whenever I think of an example of someone who engages in meaningful work, I think of Ms. Anderson, the headmistress of my primary school in South Africa. Ms. Anderson worked well into her retirement years. In my final year of school, despite being in her late seventies, she never let up. She was the first person at the school every day and the last to leave.

Like clockwork every morning, Ms. Anderson stood on the school playground to greet me as I exited the Kabal. In my final year of school, Ms. Anderson was also my teacher. My grades in primary school were terrible, a struggle I attribute to my severe nearsightedness. Eventually, my eyesight required me to sit in the front of the classroom on the floor—as close as possible to the board. The first week I was in Ms. Anderson's class, she realized I couldn't see and ensured I got glasses.

While many teachers thought I wouldn't have the grades to finish high school, let alone get into university, Ms. Anderson knew better. She took extra time at lunch and after school to help me with my homework. She encouraged me to try again when I made mistakes and patiently corrected my work until I got it right. Ms. Anderson is the reason I have five degrees today.

Even when I became class president, every week, Ms. Anderson would call me to her office to check in, and she would share suggestions for how I could get more involved in the school and support the younger kids.

My entire primary school experience was meaningful because of how Ms. Anderson connected with all her students and me. Aside from doing her job, she read the air, watching and recognizing how her students either struggled or succeeded, what motivated them, and how they were doing socially. Then she paid her actions forward by coaching, supporting, and mentoring me. Ms. Anderson had my best interests in mind, making her a better teacher, headmistress, and leader.

According to a 2014 academic study published in *Organization Science*, there are generally two ways people pay it forward. The most obvious way is for one person (like Ms. Anderson) to help another person (like me). When Ms. Anderson provided support, encouragement, and guidance, it made me feel positive about school and motivated me to help other people (like supporting the younger kids at school). We pay it forward when we help someone because that encourages them to help someone else.

But this research study also found that when you observe one person helping another person, you will reward the helpful person. So, for example, teachers who observed Ms. Anderson helping me with my homework at lunch would reward Ms. Anderson for her helpful behavior by reaching out to her and offering to teach one of her classes or mark her students' assignments. So, the more you help others, the more you build a reputation as a helpful person, which increases the likelihood that people will help you—rendering them helpful people.

Your teammates will support you if they know you have their best interests in mind. When you pay it forward, your behaviors demonstrate that you are trustworthy, which activates the rule of reciprocity. Additionally, research has shown that the more help a person receives at work, the more positive their overall behaviors are likely to be. When we help others, it decreases the likelihood our teammates will engage in negative behaviors that might be harmful to us, like harassing, discriminating, or excluding others.

The more help you receive, the more help you are likely to offer your teammates, which increases the strength of your relationships and the meaning you derive from work. When we pay it forward, we demonstrate we are trustworthy, strengthening our relationships. And the stronger your relationships are at work, the more likely you will feel connected to your workplace, which increases how meaningful your job is.

So we need to pay it forward to increase our sense of meaning at work—giving to others is, in effect, how we give to ourselves.

Finding meaning at work starts with recognizing we are part of a community. A 2014 research study published in the *Journal of Theoretical Social Psychology* found that for employees to pay it forward, they need to see themselves as members of their community at work and not as individuals. The quality of our workplace relationships plays a significant role in the meaning we derive from our work.

When you learn to read the air, you also learn how to pay it forward when it comes to the four informal processes that matter most at work: building informal networks, sharing informal information, accessing informal development, and managing your informal advancement. Knowing how to manage these four informal systems determines what we can achieve at work, but it also determines the contribution we can make—by paying it forward.

To read the air is to realize that *you are your workplace.* Your actions either contribute to building your community at work or don't. You either derive meaning from paying it forward and contributing to your community at work, or you don't. We get to determine if our work is meaningful by *how* we undertake it. When we pay forward—in how we network, share information, develop, and advance at work—we are investing in our communities, and they, in turn, invest in us.

Find a Path with Heart

On my last day of primary school, like usual, my dad dropped me off in the Kabal, and Ms. Anderson watched me take a long walk across the playground. Later that morning, she called me to her office.

"Come inside and sit down. I am meeting with some of my students to say goodbye," she said.

I felt sweat dripping down my back, dampening my school uniform. Any meeting with Ms. Anderson made me nervous; even though we had spent much time together, she was still my headmistress. I swallowed, but my mouth was dry. I tried to think of something to say.

"Ms. Anderson," I said shakily. "Would you mind signing my leaving book?" She nodded and then reached out her hand for the book.

"That's good. I actually have something for you," she said.

Instead of signing her name, Ms. Anderson turned to a blank page and began writing. I sat there for a good five minutes, wondering what she could be thinking as she scribbled furiously in my book.

Then, she paused, looked up at me with her piercing blue eyes, and smiled. Closing the book shut, she handed it back to me and said, "All the best, King. And remember . . . always keep your head up."

When I got home that day, I opened my book to see what Ms. Anderson had written.

WINDS OF FATE

A poem by Ella Wheeler Wilcox

> One ship drives east, and another drives west
> With the selfsame winds that blow.
> 'Tis the set of the sails,
> And not the gales,
> Which tells us the way to go.
> Like the winds of the seas are the ways of fate,
> As we voyage along through the life:
> 'Tis the set of a soul,
> That decides its goal,
> And not the calm or the strife.

The message from the poem Ms. Anderson gave me all those years ago applies to our careers today. As workplaces continue to change, we get to chart our course by choosing—the *set of our sail*—what gives us meaning at work. Today we are less concerned with finding a path to the top of an organizational hierarchy and more concerned with finding the path to greater meaning in the workplace, and by extension life itself.

In 1984, organizational development scholar Herb Shepard described the future of careers as "a path with heart." The protean boundaryless career offers everyone the freedom to chart their own career path—and decide how they will sail it. Your career success and fulfillment are by-products of your behavior. You get to determine the *set of your sail* by paying it forward and serving your community at work.

When we struggle to find our "path with heart," it's because we don't see how our values, needs, relationships, and workplaces have changed. Today, your formal employment contract (stipulating where and when you work) is less important than the agreement you make with yourself about how you want to manage your career and find fulfillment in your work. Your ability to find meaning at work increases your ability to find meaning in the rest of your life.

Regardless of where you work and who you work with, you can *set your sail* and make a contribution beyond *what* work you do by managing *how* you do it.

Belong Here:
Join Our Career Community

If you are interested in learning more, you can join our global career community, Belong Here, through the website www.belonghere.com.

It's free to join the community, and in doing so, you will connect with like-minded people who will support your development, advancement, and fulfillment at work. You will also be able to access our free assessment tools, development tool kits, resources, podcast, and newsletter—all of which will help you to find meaning at work.

ACKNOWLEDGMENTS

If you are reading the acknowledgments, you likely bought a copy of this book. So I would like to thank you—the reader—for spending your time, money, and energy on this book. I hope it has been helpful. I would also love to hear from you, so please feel free to reach out with your feedback, thoughts, and experiences through my website or social media—we are a community, after all.

If you thought enough of this book to buy it, then it is only fair that you know it was created in collaboration with some incredible people. First, Leila Campoli, my agent for half a decade, thank you for guiding, supporting, and advising me. Second, Michele Matrisciani, you are simply the best. Thank you for your ongoing feedback, edits, and guidance. This book would not exist without you. Third, my editors at HarperCollins, Hollis Heimbouch and Rachel Kambury, thank you for being the most supportive, enthusiastic, and encouraging editors. I am so grateful I got to work on this with both of you. Finally, I would also like to thank Carmel Clarkin for her research support and Carol Rosenberg for her formatting support.

Creating a research-based nonfiction book is a long, slow process, much like training for a marathon. To survive the process and enjoy it, you need a community. So I would like to thank mine. To my family, friends, and all the people I have worked with, thank you for your love and support. You make my work worth doing. Finally, to my business partner, Selina Suresh, we did it. Thank you for be-lieving in me enough to try and for keeping up your end of the trust exchange.

This book is what I am leaving behind, and I am so grateful that I was brave enough to believe that workplaces can work differently. I hope that you—the reader—find yourself in this book and are daring enough to choose a "path with heart" and decide for yourself what you will leave behind.

NOTES

PREFACE

ix   In the Fishlake National Forest: Marnie Chesterton, "The Oldest Living Thing on Earth," *BBC News*, June 12, 2017, https://www.bbc.co.uk/news/science-environment-40224991.

ix   The oldest quaking aspen: Wikipedia, "Pando (Tree)," accessed September 28, 2022, https://en.wikipedia.org/wiki/Pando_(tree)#:~:text=Size%20and%2age,-The%20clonal%20colony&text=The%20root%20system%20is%20estimated,Pando%20are%20approaching%20this%20limit.

ix   Researchers initially believed: Ferris Jabr, "The Social Life of Forests," *New York Times*, December 2, 2020, https://www.nytimes.com/interactive/2020/12/02/magazine/tree-communication-mycorrhiza.html.

x   Over an average lifetime: Leigh Campbell, "We've Broken Down Your Entire Life into Years Spent Doing Tasks," *Huffington Post*, updated October 19, 2017, https://www.huffingtonpost.co.uk/entry/weve-broken-down-your-entire-life-into-years-spent-doing-tasks_n_61087617e4b0999d2084fec5.

INTRODUCTION

xiii A businessman in Kyoto: だーます (@dms9000), "During a business meeting with a company in Kyoto, I was told, 'You have a good watch,' and I told him about the specs of the watch. How I felt when I realized that my true intentions were actually sarcastic, saying, 'Let's talk for a long time,'" Twitter post, August 21, 2019, https://twitter.com/dms9000/status/1164380597990543360?ref_src=twsrcpercent5Etfwpercent7Ctwcamppercent5Etweetembedpercent7Ctwtermpercent5E1164380597990543360percent7Ctwgrpercent5Epercent7Ctwconpercent5Es1_&ref_url=httpspercent3Apercent2Fpercent2Fsoranews24.compercent2F2019percent2F08percent2F27percent2Fin-kyoto-hey-youve-got-a-really-nice-watch-is-not-a-compliment-japanese-businessman-sayspercent2F.

xiv The Japanese have a term: Bryan Lufkin, "How 'Reading the Air' Keeps Japan Running," BBC, January 29, 2020, https://www.bbc.com/worklife/article/20200129-what-is-reading-the-air-in-japan.

xv In an old Zen story: Buddha Groove, "Zen Story: Which Side?" *Balance by Buddha Groove* blog, accessed September 1, 2022, https://blog.buddhagroove.com/zen-story-which-side/.

xvi Automation, AI, and universal interconnectivity: Zlatko Skrbiš and Jacqueline Laughland-Booÿ, "Technology, Change, and Uncertainty: Maintaining Career Confidence in the Early 21st Century," *New Technology, Work and Employment* 34, no. 3 (October 2019): 191–207, https://doi.org/10.1111/ntwe.12151.

xvi Complex, critical tasks: Sadhna Dash, "Rewriting the HR Playbook for the Future," *NHRD Network Journal* 13, no. 4 (October 2020): 442–53, https://doi.org/10.1177/2631454120963406.

xvi in a Fanuc plant: FANUC, "FANUC Produces 750,000th Robot," July 2021, accessed September 4, 2022, https://www.fanuc.eu/es/en/who-we-are/news/eu-750k-robots-07-2021.

xvi Before the pandemic, it was widely agreed: Skrbiš and Laughland-Booÿ, "Technology, Change, and Uncertainty."

xvi The Hopes and Fears 2021 report: PwC Global, "Hopes and Fears 2021: The Views of 32,500 Workers," accessed September 1, 2022, https://www.pwc.com /gx/en/issues/upskilling/hopes-and-fears.html.

xvii In 2021, approximately: Susan Lund, Anu Madgavkar, James Manyika, Sven Smit, Kweilin Ellingrud, and Olivia Robinson, "The Future of Work After COVID-19," McKinsey Global Institute, February 18, 2021, https://www .mckinsey.com/featured-insights/future-of-work/the-future-of-work-after -covid-19.

xviii specialist technical roles: Matthew Sigelman, Scott Bittle, Will Markow, and Benjamin Francis, "The Hybrid Job Economy: How New Skills Are Rewriting the DNA of the Job Market," Burning Glass Technologies, accessed September 1, 2022, https://www.burning-glass.com/wp-content/uploads/hybrid _jobs_2019_final.pdf.

xviii They require a wide range of skills: Ibid.

xix By 2030, the World Economic Forum: Robert van Eerd and Jean Guo, "Jobs Will Be Very Different in 10 Years. Here's How to Prepare," World Economic Forum, January 17, 2020, https://www.weforum.org/agenda/2020/01/future-of-work/.

xix As a result of the pandemic: Prithwiraj (Raj) Choudhury, "Our Work-from-Anywhere Future," *Harvard Business Review* (November–December 2020), https://hbr.org/2020/11/our-work-from-anywhere-future.

xx population of multiracial and racial and ethnic minorities: Sandra L. Colby and Jennifer M. Ortman, "Projections of the Size and Composition of the U.S. Population: 2014 to 2060," U.S. Census Bureau, March 2015, accessed September 1, 2022, https://www.census.gov/content/dam/Census/library/publica-tions/2015/demo/p25-1143.pdf.

xx by 2044, more than half of all Americans: Ibid.

xx demand is expected to grow: Jacques Bughin, Eric Hazan, Susan Lund, Peter Dahlström, Anna Wiesinger, and Amresh Subramaniam, "Skill Shift: Automa-tion and the Future of the Workforce," McKinsey Global Institute, May 23, 2018, https://www.mckinsey.com/featured-insights/future-of-work/skill-shift -automation-and-the-future-of-the-workforce.

xxi 2021 McKinsey survey: Andrea Alexander, Rich Cracknell, Aaron De Smet, Meredith Langstaff, Mihir Mysore, and Dan Ravid, "What Executives Are Say-ing About the Future of Hybrid Work," McKinsey Global Institute, May 17, 2021, https://www.mckinsey.com/business-functions/people-and-organizational -performance/our-insights/what-executives-are-saying-about-the-future-of -hybrid-work.

xxii global study conducted in 2021: Steelcase, "Changing Expectations and the Future of Work," Steelcase Global Report 2021, accessed September 1, 2022, https://www.steelcase.com/content/uploads/2021/02/2021_AM_SC_Global -Report_Changing-Expectations-and-the-Future-of-Work-2.pdf.

xxii In a 2021 survey: Aaron De Smet, Bonnie Dowling, Mihir Mysore, and An-gelika Reich, "It's Time for Leaders to Get Real About Hybrid," McKinsey Global Institute, July 9, 2021, https://www.mckinsey.com/business-functions /people-and-organizational-performance/our-insights/its-time-for-leaders -to-get-real-about-hybrid.

xxii Collaboration became harder virtually: Aaron De Smet, Mihir Mysore, Angelika Reich, and Bob Sternfels, "Return as a Muscle: How Lessons from COVID-19 Can Shape a Robust Operating Model for Hybrid and Beyond," McKinsey Global Institute, July 9, 2021, https://www.mckinsey.com/business-functions /people-and-organizational-performance/our-insights/return-as-a-muscle -how-lessons-from-covid-19-can-shape-a-robust-operating-model-for-hybrid -and-beyond.

xxii Hybrid work makes it harder: Ibid.

xxii A 2020 Boston Consulting Group survey: Adriana Dahik, Deborah Lovich, Caroline Kreafle, Allison Bailey, Julie Kilmann, Derek Kennedy, Prateek Roongta, Felix Schuler, Leo Tomlin, and John Wenstrup, "What 12,000 Employees Have to Say About the Future of Remote Work," BCG, August 11, 2020, https://www.bcg.com/publications/2020/valuable-productivity-gains-covid-19.

xxiii mental health issues and burnout increased: De Smet et al., "Return as a Muscle."

xxiii Only 14 percent of executives: Dahik et al., "What 12,000 Employees Have to Say About the Future of Remote Work."

xxiv The 2018 study: Evi De Bruyne and Doranne Gerritse, "Exploring the Future Workplace: Results of the Futures Forum Study," *Journal of Corporate Real Estate* 20, no. 4 (October 2018): 196–213, https://doi.org/10.1108/JCRE-09-2017-0030.

xxiv Employees will have to manage: Ibid.

xxiv Given the critical need: Peter O'Connor and Karen Becker, "As Work Gets More Ambiguous, Younger Generations May Be Less Equipped for It," *Conversationist*, January 21, 2019, https://theconversation.com/as-work-gets-more-ambiguous-younger-generations-may-be-less-equipped-for-it-105674#:~:text=Youngerpercent20workerspercent20showpercent20lesspercent20capacity,lifepercent20eventspercent20topercent20drawpercent20from.

xxv a 2019 study: Ibid.

xxviii *Harvard Business Review* found: Tensie Whelan and Randi Kronthal-Sacco, "Research: Actually, Consumers Do Buy Sustainable Products," *Harvard Business Review* (June 19, 2019), https://hbr.org/2019/06/research-actually-consumers-do-buy-sustainable-products?registration=success.

xxviii Nielsen Global Corporate Sustainability Report: Ashton Manufacturing, "66% of Consumers Willing to Pay More for Sustainable Goods, Nielsen Report Reveals," accessed September 1, 2022, https://ashtonmanufacturing.com.au/66-of-consumers-willing-to-pay-more-for-sustainable-goods-nielsen-report-reveals/.

xxviii Employees want employers to focus: Tim Minahan, "What Your Future Employees Want Most," *Harvard Business Review* (May 3, 2021), https://hbr.org/2021/05/what-your-future-employees-want-most.

xxix A 2014 research study: Ivy Kyei-Poku, "The Benefits of Belongingness and Interactional Fairness to Interpersonal Citizenship Behavior," *Leadership & Organization Development Journal* 35, no. 8 (2014): 691–709, https://psycnet.apa.org/doi/10.1108/LODJ-09-2012-0117.

xxx research conducted in 2021: Jacques Bughin, Eric Hazan, Susan Lund, Peter Dahlström, Anna Wiesinger, and Amresh Subramaniam, "Skill Shift: Automation and the Future of the Workforce," McKinsey Global Institute, May 23, 2018, https://www.mckinsey.com/featured-insights/future-of-work/skill-shift-automation-and-the-future-of-the-workforce.

xxx A 2008 research study: Laura Sabattini, "Unwritten Rules: What You Don't Know Can Hurt Your Career," Catalyst, June 15, 2008, https://www.catalyst.org/research/unwritten-rules-what-you-dont-know-can-hurt-your-career/.

xxxi A 2010 study by Catalyst: Laura Sabattini and Sarah Dinolfo, "Unwritten Rules: Why Doing a Good Job Might Not Be Enough," Catalyst, February 9, 2010, https://www.catalyst.org/research/unwritten-rules-why-doing-a-good-job-might-not-be-enough/.

xxxi Nintendo Switch released the game: Chad Soriano, "Kuukiyomi: Consider It Gameplay (Nintendo Switch)," December 21, 2019, accessed September 1, 2022, video, 12:47, https://www.youtube.com/watch?v=JqNaEgWdRgc.

xxxiii   the 2008 research study by Catalyst: Sabattini, "Unwritten Rules: What You Don't Know Can Hurt Your Career."

xxxvi   A 2021 online survey: Monster, "Fall 2021 Hiring Report," accessed September 1, 2022, https://media.monster.com/marketing/2021/Monster-2021-Fall -Hiring-Report.pdf.

xxxvii   The 2017 Pearson report: Hasan Bakhshi, Jonathan M. Downing, Michael A. Osborne, and Philippe Schneider, *The Future of Skills: Employment in 2030* (London: Pearson and Nesta, 2017).

CHAPTER 1: A PLACE TO STAND: HOW TO BELONG

3   As humans, our longing: Roy F. Baumeister and Mark R. Leary, "The Need to Belong: Desire for Interpersonal Attachments as a Fundamental Human Motivation," *Psychological Bulletin* 117, no. 3 (1995): 497–529, http://persweb.wabash .edu/facstaff/hortonr/articles%20for%20class/baumeister%20and%20 leary.pdf.

3   The belonging hypothesis: Ibid.

3   studies consistently find: Ibid.

3   the part of our brain: Lee Waller, "Fostering a Sense of Belonging in the Workplace: Enhancing Well-Being and a Positive and Coherent Sense of Self," in *The Palgrave Handbook of Workplace Well-Being*, ed. Satinder Dhiman (London: Palgrave Macmillan, 2021), 341–67.

3   it is worse to be isolated: Jane O'Reilly, Sandra L. Robinson, Jennifer L. Berdahl, and Sara Banki, "Is Negative Attention Better than No Attention? The Comparative Effects of Ostracism and Harassment at Work," *Organization Science* 26, no. 3 (May–June 2015): 774–93, https://www.sauder.ubc.ca/sites/default /files/2019-07/Oreilly%20et%20al%20Org%20Sci.pdf.

4   a survey by the consulting firm EY: Karyn Twaronite, "Op-Ed: Connected, Yet Lacking Connections: How We Can Combat Loneliness at Work," CNBC, February 25, 2022, https://www.cnbc.com/2022/02/25/op-ed-connected-yet-few -connections-how-we-combat-work-loneliness.html.

4   When employees feel: Archana Ramesh, "Why Belonging Is Important at Work: Employee Engagement and Diversity," *Glint*, April 23, 2020, https://www.glint-inc.com/blog/why-belonging-is-important-at-work-employee-engagement -and-diversity/.

4   2019 *Harvard Business Review* study: Evan W. Carr, Andrew Reece, Gabriella Rosen Kellerman, and Alexi Robichaux, "The Value of Belonging at Work," *Harvard Business Review* (December 16, 2019), https://hbr.org/2019/12/the-value -of-belonging-at-work.

4   being ignored by your colleagues: Ibid.

4   isolation is becoming even more difficult: Ibid.

5   lack of belonging also contributes: Julianne Holt-Lunstad, Timothy B. Smith, Mark Baker, Tyler Harris, and David Stephenson, "Loneliness and Social Isolation as Risk Factors for Mortality: A Meta-Analytic Review," *Perspectives on Psychological Science* 10, no. 2 (March 2015): 227–37, http://doi .org/10.1177/1745691614568352.

5   A 2021 study examining the experiences: CEO Monthly, "Over 50% of Remote Workers Are Worried About Workplace Exclusion," April 28, 2021, https://www .ceo-review.com/over-50-of-remote-workers-are-worried-about-workplace -exclusion/.

7   research undertaken by Kate Davey: Kate Mackenzie Davey, "Women's Accounts of Organizational Politics as a Gendering Process," *Gender, Work & Organization* 15, no. 6 (2008): 650–71, https://doi.org/10.1111/j.1468-0432.2008.00420.x.

9   A 2019 research study: Courtney L. McCluney and Verónica Caridad Rabelo,

"Conditions of Visibility: An Intersectional Examination of Black Women's Belongingness and Distinctiveness at Work," *Journal of Vocational Behavior* 113 (2019): 143–52, https://doi.org/10.1016/j.jvb.2018.09.008.

10 study by the consulting firm Glint: Ramesh, "Why Belonging Is Important at Work: Employee Engagement and Diversity."

11 study examining employees' experiences: Lee Waller, "Sense of Not Belonging at Work," Ashridge Hult Research Report, 2020, accessed September 1, 2022, https://www.hultef.com/en/insights/research-thought-leadership/research-sense-not-belonging-work.

12 A study published in 2004: Stephen Billett, "Co-Participation at Work: Learning Through Work and Throughout Working Lives," *Studies in the Education of Adults* 36, no. 2 (2004): 190–205, https://doi.org/10.1080/02660830.2004.11661496.

13 *Diversity Wins: How Inclusion Matters* report: Vivian Hunt, Sara Prince, Sundiatu Dixon-Fyle, and Kevin Dolan, "Diversity Wins: How Inclusion Matters," McKinsey & Company, 2020, accessed September 1, 2022, https://www.mckinsey.com/~/media/mckinsey/featured%20insights/diversity%20and%20inclusion/diversity%20wins%20how%20inclusion%20matters/diversity-wins-how-inclusion-matters-vf.pdf.

13 when employees are excluded from their colleagues: Susan Sorenson and Keri Garman, "How to Tackle U.S. Employees' Stagnating Engagement," Gallup, June 11, 2013, https://news.gallup.com/businessjournal/162953/tackle-employees-stagnating-engagement.aspx.

14 The average American workweek: Derek Thompson, "Workism Is Making Americans Miserable," *Atlantic*, February 24, 2019, https://www.theatlantic.com/ideas/archive/2019/02/religion-workism-making-americans-miserable/583441/.

17 nineteen million American workers: Aaron De Smet, Bonnie Dowling, Marino Mugayar-Baldocchi, and Bill Schaninger, "'Great Attrition' or 'Great Attraction'? The Choice Is Yours," McKinsey & Company, September 8, 2021, https://www.mckinsey.com/business-functions/people-and-organizational-performance/our-insights/great-attrition-or-great-attraction-the-choice-is-yours.

17 A 2021 McKinsey study: Ibid.

19 on DEI initiatives: McKinsey & Company, "Focusing on What Works for Workplace Diversity," April 7, 2017, video, 5:48, https://www.mckinsey.com/featured-insights/gender-equality/focusing-on-what-works-for-workplace-diversity.

19 estimated that 40 percent of employees: Karyn Twaronite, "The Surprising Power of Simply Asking Coworkers How They're Doing," *Harvard Business Review* (February 28, 2019), https://hbr.org/2019/02/the-surprising-power-of-simply-asking-coworkers-how-theyre-doing.

19 2018 *State of Diversity Report*: Atlassian, "State of Diversity and Inclusion in U.S. Tech: Stats Summary, March 2018," accessed September 1, 2022, https://www.atlassian.com/dam/jcr:c009637c-1335–429d-9181–6a66685b712e/Atlassian_StateofDiversityTech_2018_StatsSummary.pdf.

20 Deloitte surveyed 245 companies: PR Newswire, "New Deloitte Research Identifies Keys to Creating Fair and Inclusive Organizations," May 10, 2017, https://www.prnewswire.com/news-releases/new-deloitte-research-identifies-keys-to-creating-fair-and-inclusive-organizations-300455164.html.

CHAPTER 2: THE TRUST EXCHANGE: HOW TO READ THE AIR

28 According to a 2020 Edelman survey: Edelman, "2019 Edelman Trust Barometer: Executive Summary," accessed September 3, 2022, https://www.edelman.com/sites/g/files/aatuss191/files/2019-02/2019_Edelman_Trust_Barometer_Executive_Summary.pdf.

28   Research has found that low levels of trust in workplaces: Frances Alston and Donald Tippett, "Does a Technology-Driven Organization's Culture Influence the Trust Employees Have in Their Managers?" *Engineering Management Journal* 21, no. 2 (2009): 3–10, http://doi.org/10.1080/10429247.2009.11431801.

29   A 2017 study: De Bruyne and Gerritse, "Exploring the Future Workplace: Results of the Futures Forum Study."

29   a range of beneficial outcomes: Paul J. Zak, "The Neuroscience of Trust: Management Behaviors That Foster Employee Engagement," *Harvard Business Review* (January–February 2017), https://hbr.org/2017/01/the-neuroscience-of-trust.

30   employees who trust their organizations: Ibid.

30   PricewaterhouseCoopers reported: PwC, "19th Annual Global CEO Survey, January 2016: Redefining Business Success in a Changing World," accessed September 3, 2022, https://www.pwc.com/ee/et/publications/CEOSurvey/pwc-19th-annual-global-ceo-survey.pdf.

31   the top three reasons: Karyn Twaronite, "Five Findings on the Importance of Belonging," Ernst & Young Global Limited, May 11, 2019, https://www.ey.com/en_us/diversity-inclusiveness/ey-belonging-barometer-workplace-study.

31   50 percent less likely to leave: Gabriella Rosen Kellerman and Andrew Reece, "The Value of Belonging at Work: Investing in Workplace Inclusion," BetterUp, accessed September 3, 2022, https://grow.betterup.com/resources/the-value-of-belonging-at-work-the-business-case-for-investing-in-workplace-inclusion-event.

31   when people are treated fairly: Joshua R. Knapp, Therese A. Sprinkle, Michael J. Urick, and Kelly A. Delaney-Klinger, "The Belonging Model of Trust," *Nonprofit Management and Leadership* 30, no. 1 (May 2019): 133–53, https://doi.org/10.1002/nml.21370.

32   a 2004 academic study: Kim S. Cameron, David Bright, and Arran Caza, "Exploring the Relationships Between Organizational Virtuousness and Performance," *American Behavioral Scientist* 47, no. 6 (February 2004): 766–90, https://doi.org/10.1177/0002764203260209.

32   a 2016 study: Edelman, "2022 Edelman Trust Barometer," accessed September 28, 2022, https://www.edelman.com/trust/2022-trust-barometer/special-report-trust-workplace.

32   today's hybrid workplace: Cameron et al., "Exploring the Relationships Between Organizational Virtuousness and Performance."

33   virtual working limits our ability: Kaisa Henttonen and Kirsimarja Blomqvist, "Managing Distance in a Global Virtual Team: The Evolution of Trust Through Technology-Mediated Relational Communication," *Strategic Change* 14, no. 2 (April 2005): 107–19, https://doi.org/10.1002/jsc.714.

33   A 2005 academic study: Ibid.

36   *Asia Pacific Management Review* states: Lalatendu Kesari Jena, Sajeet Pradhan, and Nrusingh Prasad Panigrahy, "Pursuit of Organisational Trust: Role of Employee Engagement, Psychological Well-Being and Transformational Leadership," *Asia Pacific Management Review* 23, no. 3 (August 2018): 227–34, http://doi.org/10.1016/j.apmrv.2017.11.001.

37   *Personnel Psychology* reviewed relevant literature: In-Sue Oh, Russell P. Guay, Kwanghyun Kim, Crystal M. Harold, Jong-Hyun Lee, Chang-Goo Heo, and Kang-Hyun Shin, "Fit Happens Globally: A Meta-Analytic Comparison of the Relationships of Person–Environment Fit Dimensions with Work Attitudes and Performance Across East Asia, Europe, and North America," *Personnel Psychology* 67, no. 1 (Spring 2014): 99–152, https://doi.org/10.1111/peps.12026.

37   When you identify: Ibid.

38   Research has found that demonstrating sensitivity: Frances Alston and Donald

Tippett, "Does a Technology-Driven Organization's Culture Influence the Trust Employees Have in Their Managers?" *Engineering Management Journal* 21, no. 2 (2009): 3–10, DOI:10.1080/10429247.2009.11431801.

38 the most successful managers: Scott E. Seibert, Maria L. Kraimer, and Robert C. Liden, "A Social Capital Theory of Career Success," *Academy of Management Journal* 44, no. 2 (April 2001): 219–37, DOI:10.2307/3069452.

38 70 percent of all jobs: Julia Freeland Fisher, "How to Get a Job Often Comes Down to One Elite Personal Asset, and Many People Still Don't Realize It," CNBC, December 27, 2019, https://www.cnbc.com/2019/12/27/how-to-get-a -job-often-comes-down-to-one-elite-personal-asset.html.

39 A 2013 research study: M. Max Evans, "Is Trust the Most Important Human Factor Influencing Knowledge Sharing in Organisations?" *Journal of Information & Knowledge Management* 12, no. 4 (2013): 1–17, https://doi.org/10.1142 /S021964921350038X.

40 Research has firmly established: David R. Hekman, Gregory A. Bigley, Kevin Steensma, and James Hereford, "Combined Effects of Organizational and Professional Identification on the Reciprocity Dynamic for Professional Employees," *Academy of Management Journal* 52, no. 3 (June 2009): 506–26, http://doi .org/10.5465/AMJ.2009.41330897.

41 Career advocates matter: Sylvia Ann Hewlett, Kerrie Peraino, Laura Sherbin, and Karen Sumberg, *The Sponsor Effect: Breaking Through the Last Glass Ceiling* (Boston: *Harvard Business Review*, 2010).

46 A 1997 study: Deepa Narayan and Lant Pritchett, "Cents and Sociability: Household Income and Social Capital in Rural Tanzania," *Economic Development and Cultural Change* 47, no. 4 (July 1999): 871–97, https://doi .org/10.1086/452436.

46 Researchers examining social capital: Felix Requena, "Social Capital, Satisfaction and Quality of Life in the Workplace," *Social Indicators Research* 61, no. 3 (March 2003): 331–60, https://doi.org/10.1023/A:1021923520951.

CHAPTER 3: INFORMAL NETWORKS: HOW TO GAIN CAREER-DEFINING ADVICE AND SUPPORT

49 three decades of research: Gail M. McGuire and William T. Bielby, "The Variable Effects of Tie Strength and Social Resources: How Type of Support Matters," *Work and Occupations* 43, no. 1 (August 2015): 38–74, https://doi .org/10.1177/0730888415596560.

49 A 2016 research study: Jessica R. Methot, Jeffery A. Lepine, Nathan P. Podsakoff, and Jessica Siegel Christian, "Are Workplace Friendships a Mixed Blessing? Exploring Tradeoffs of Multiplex Relationships and Their Associations with Job Performance," *Personnel Psychology* 69, no. 2 (April 2015): 311–55, https://doi .org/10.1111/peps.12109.

50 Employees with close relationships: Ibid.

51 thanks to hybrid working: Marissa King and Balázs Kovács, "Research: We're Losing Touch with Our Networks," *Harvard Business Review* (February 12, 2021), https://hbr.org/2021/02/research-were-losing-touch-with-our-networks.

51 a 2011 research study: Ibid.

51 a 2012 research study: LinkedIn Corporate Communications, "Eighty-Percent of Professionals Consider Networking Important to Career Success," LinkedIn Pressroom, June 22, 2017, https://news.linkedin.com/2017/6/eighty-percent -of-professionals-consider-networking-important-to-career-success.

52 employees will change their jobs: Suzanne C. de Janasz, Sherry E. Sullivan, and Vicki Whiting, "Networks and Career Success: Lessons for Turbulent Times,"

Academy of Management Perspectives 17, no. 4 (November 2003): 78–91, https://www.jstor.org/stable/4166008.

52   A 2013 research study: Michael Simmons, "The No. 1 Predictor of Career Success According to Network Science," *Forbes*, January 15, 2015, https://www.forbes.com/sites/michaelsimmons/2015/01/15/this-is-the-1-predictor-of-career-success-according-to-network-science/?sh=6bfde549e829.

53   a 2002 *MIT Sloan Management Review*: Rob Cross, Nitin Nohria, and Andrew Parker, "Six Myths About Informal Networks—and How to Overcome Them," *MIT Sloan Management Review* 43, no. 3 (April 2002): 67, https://sloanreview.mit.edu/article/six-myths-about-informal-networks-and-how-to-overcome-them/.

54   more access to information: Ibid.

56   Information is communicated: Keith Davis, "Grapevine Communication Among Lower and Middle Managers," *Personnel Journal* 48, no. 4 (April 1969): 269–72.

56   research has found that supervisors: Jitendra Mishra, "Managing the Grapevine," *Public Personnel Management* 19, no. 2 (June 1990): 213–28, https://doi.org/10.1177/009102609001900209.

57   In 1932: Jonathan D. Moreno, "Social Networking Didn't Start at Harvard," *Slate*, October 21, 2014, https://slate.com/technology/2014/10/j-l-moreno-a-psychologists-30s-experiments-invented-social-networking.html.

57   a 2014 article published in *Slate*: Ibid.

60   According to a 2017 study: Rob Cross and Robert Thomas, "Managing Yourself: A Smarter Way to Network," *Harvard Business Review* (July–August 2011), https://hbr.org/2011/07/managing-yourself-a-smarter-way-to-network.

61   a 2005 research study: Brian Uzzi and Shannon Dunlap, "How to Build Your Network," *Harvard Business Review* 83, no. 12 (December 2005): 53, https://hbr.org/2005/12/how-to-build-your-network.

61   The more diverse a network: Dawn E. Chanland and Wendy Marcinkus Murphy, "Propelling Diverse Leaders to the Top: A Developmental Network Approach," *Human Resource Management* 57, no. 1 (September 2017): 111–26, https://doi.org/10.1002/hrm.21842.

63   A 2013 study: Linus Dahlander and Daniel A. McFarland, "Ties That Last: Tie Formation and Persistence in Research Collaborations over Time," *Administrative Science Quarterly* 58, no. 1 (January 2013): 69–110, https://doi.org/10.1177/0001839212474272.

63   improve work performance: John Paul Stephens, Emily Heaphy, and Jane E. Dutton, "High-Quality Connections," in *The Oxford Handbook of Positive Organizational Scholarship*, eds. Kim S. Cameron and Gretchen M. Spreitzer (New York: Oxford University Press, 2012), 385–99.

63   Quality relationships: Dahlander and McFarland, "Ties That Last."

64   a 2011 study: Cross and Thomas, "Managing Yourself."

64   high-quality relationships: Jane E. Dutton and Emily D. Heaphy, "The Power of High-Quality Connections," in *Positive Organizational Scholarship: Foundations of a New Discipline* (San Francisco: Berrett-Koehler, 2003), 263–78.

65   A 2012 research study: Rob Cross, Kevin Oakes, and Connor Cross, "Cultivating an Inclusive Culture Through Personal Networks," *MIT Sloan Management Review* (June 8, 2021), https://sloanreview.mit.edu/article/cultivating-an-inclusive-culture-through-personal-networks/.

66   Consistently, research has found: Wayne Baker and Jane E. Dutton, "Enabling Positive Social Capital in Organizations: Building a Theoretical and Research Foundation," in *Exploring Positive Relationships at Work: Building a Theoretical and Research Foundation* (New York: Lawrence Erlbaum Associates, 2007), 325–46.

66 demographic diversity matters: Marco D'Errico, Silvana Stefani, and Anna Tor-
    riero, "Informal Ties in Organizations: A Case Study," *Quality & Quantity* 48, no.
    4 (July 2014): 1929–43, https://doi.org/10.1007/s11135-013-9862-0.

66 a 2016 study: McGuire and Bielby, "The Variable Effects of Tie Strength and So-
    cial Resources."

67 loose ties are more helpful: Suzanne C. de Janasz and Monica L. Forret, "Learn-
    ing the Art of Networking: A Critical Skill for Enhancing Social Capital and
    Career Success," *Journal of Management Education* 32, no. 5 (October 2008):
    629–50, https://doi.org/10.1177/1052562907307637.

67 A 2018 study: Chanland and Murphy, "Propelling Diverse Leaders to the Top: A
    Developmental Network Approach."

71 2019 study *Social Capital and Career Growth*: Dae-seok Kang, Jeff Gold, Jeon-
    geun Kim, and Ilsoo Kim, "Social Capital and Career Growth," *International
    Journal of Manpower* 41, no. 1 (September 2019): 100–116, http://doi.org/10.1108
    /ijm-10-2018-0345.

72 an article in the *Guardian*: Hunter Felt, "Is Anything More Stupid than Base-
    ball's Unwritten Rules? Ask Fernando Tatis Jr," *The Guardian*, August 19, 2020,
    https://www.theguardian.com/sport/2020/aug/19/fernando-tatis-jr-grand
    -slam-take-sign-baseball-anger-unwritten-rules.

CHAPTER 4: INFORMAL INFORMATION: HOW TO BE IN THE KNOW

76 people are self-aware: Dan Moshavi, F. William Brown, and Nancy G. Dodd,
    "Leader Self-Awareness and Its Relationship to Subordinate Attitudes and Per-
    formance," *Leadership & Organization Development Journal* 24, no. 7 (Novem-
    ber 2003): 407–18, https://doi.org/10.1108/01437730310498622.

77 Self-awareness enables: Paul J. Silvia and Maureen E. O'Brien, "Self-Awareness
    and Constructive Functioning: Revisiting 'the Human Dilemma,'" *Journal
    of Social and Clinical Psychology* 23, no. 4 (August 2004): 475–89, https://doi
    .org/10.1521/jscp.23.4.475.40307.

78 a 2012 academic research study: Stephens et al., "High-Quality Connections,"
    385–99.

78 Other awareness: Ibid.

79 When we have to collaborate: Mark Mortensen and Tsedal B. Neeley, "Reflected
    Knowledge and Trust in Global Collaboration," *Management Science* 58, no. 12
    (July 2012): 2207–24, https://doi.org/10.1287/mnsc.1120.1546.

79 In a virtual setting: Michael Eraut, "Non-Formal Learning and Tacit Knowl-
    edge in Professional Work," *British Journal of Educational Psychology* 70, no. 1
    (2000): 113–36, http://doi.org/10.1348/000709900158001.

79 Judgments are sticky: Ibid.

80 when distant employees: Mortensen and Neeley, "Reflected Knowledge and
    Trust in Global Collaboration."

80 organizational awareness: Ibid.

81 We need organizational awareness: Stephens et al., "High-Quality Connec-
    tions," 385–99.

82 the human resources team: Hofstede Insights, "What About the UK?" accessed
    September 28, 2022, https://www.hofstede-insights.com/country/the-uk/.

82 Collaboration is king: Rob Cross, Greg Pryor, and David Sylvester, "How to Suc-
    ceed Quickly in a New Role: Five Ways to Build a Strategic Network," *Harvard
    Business Review* (November–December 2021), https://hbr.org/2021/11/how-to
    -succeed-quickly-in-a-new-role.

82 a 2021 research study: Ibid.

83 Remote working: Ibid.

83 Misunderstandings arise: Mortensen and Neeley, "Reflected Knowledge and Trust in Global Collaboration."

84 Organizational awareness improves: T. Northup, "Awareness: The Key Insight for Organizational Change," 2007, www.lmgsuccess.com/documents/awareness.pdf.

84 One of my first jobs: Eben Harrell, "A Brief History of Personality Tests," *Harvard Business Review* (March–April 2017), https://hbr.org/2017/03/a-brief-history-of-personality-tests#:~:text=Since%20the%201960s%2C%20some%2050,popular%20personality%20assessment%20ever%20created.

85 a gap exists: Moshavi et al., "Leader Self-Awareness and Its Relationship to Subordinate Attitudes and Performance."

85 a 2018 study: Tasha Eurich, "Working with People Who Aren't Self-Aware," *Harvard Business Review* (October 19, 2018), https://hbr.org/2018/10/working-with-people-who-arent-self-aware.

86 people generally fall: Moshavi et al., "Leader Self-Awareness and Its Relationship to Subordinate Attitudes and Performance."

87 a 2015 *Harvard Business Review* study: Erich C. Dierdorff and Robert S. Rubin, "Research: We're Not Very Self-Aware, Especially at Work," *Harvard Business Review* (March 12, 2015), https://hbr.org/2015/03/research-were-not-very-self-aware-especially-at-work.

87 doesn't improve on its own: Moshavi et al., "Leader Self-Awareness and Its Relationship to Subordinate Attitudes and Performance."

87 the CEO disease: Fabio Sala, "Executive Blind Spots: Discrepancies Between Self- and Other-Ratings," *Consulting Psychology Journal: Practice and Research* 55, no. 4 (September 2003): 222–29, http://doi.org/10.1037/1061-4087.55.4.222.

87 80 percent of senior executives: J. Evelyn Orr, "Proof Point: Survival of the Most Self-Aware: Nearly 80 Percent of Leaders Have Blind Spots About Their Skills," The Korn/Ferry Institute, 2012, accessed September 3, 2022, https://www.kornferry.com/content/dam/kornferry/docs/article-migration/Survival%20of%20the%20most%20self-aware-%20Nearly%2080%20percent%20of%20leaders%20have%20blind%20spots%20about%20their%20skills%20.pdf.

87 revenue, profitability, and competitive advantage: Northup, "Awareness."

88 underestimators may struggle: Tomas Chamorro-Premuzic, "Why Do So Many Incompetent Men Become Leaders?" *Harvard Business Review* (August 22, 2013), https://hbr.org/2013/08/why-do-so-many-incompetent-men.

88 have a high degree of self-awareness: Moshavi et al., "Leader Self-Awareness and Its Relationship to Subordinate Attitudes and Performance."

88 the more self-aware you are: Anna Sutton, Helen M. Williams, and Christopher W. Allinson, "A Longitudinal, Mixed Method Evaluation of Self-Awareness Training in the Workplace," *European Journal of Training and Development* 39, no. 7 (August 2015): 610–27, https://doi.org/10.1108/EJTD-04-2015-0031.

89 regarding team performance: Erich C. Dierdorff, David M. Fisher, and Robert S. Rubin, "The Power of Percipience: Consequences of Self-Awareness in Teams on Team-Level Functioning and Performance," *Journal of Management* 45, no. 7 (2019): 2891–919, https://doi.org/10.1177/0149206318774622.

89 self-awareness enables creativity: Silvia and O'Brien, "Self-Awareness and Constructive Functioning."

89 a determinant of organizational success: Michael O'Callaghan, Chris Campbell, David Zes, and Dana Landis, "A Better Return on Self-Awareness," Korn Ferry Advance, accessed September 3, 2022, https://www.kornferry.com/institute/647-a-better-return-on-self-awareness.

92 Research published in the 2018: Tasha Eurich, "What Self-Awareness Really Is

(and How to Cultivate It)," *Harvard Business Review* (January 4, 2018), https://hbr.org/2018/01/what-self-awareness-really-is-and-how-to-cultivate-it.

92 another *Harvard Business Review* study: Giada Di Stefano, Francesca Gino, Gary P. Pisano, and Bradley R. Staats, "Making Experience Count: The Role of Reflection in Individual Learning," Harvard Business School NOM Unit Working Paper 14–093 (2016), accessed September 3, 2022, https://papers.ssrn.com/sol3/papers.cfm?abstract_id=2414478.

93 make reflection a regular practice: Sutton et al., "A Longitudinal, Mixed Method Evaluation of Self-Awareness Training in the Workplace."

93 A 2014 research study: Paul M. Leonardi, "Social Media, Knowledge Sharing, and Innovation: Toward a Theory of Communication Visibility," *Information Systems Research* 25, no. 4 (October 2014): 796–816, https://doi.org/10.1287/isre.2014.0536.

94 reduced work visibility: Ibid.

95 Most of us hate: Jinseok Chun, Joel Brockner, and David De Cremer, "People Don't Want to Be Compared with Others in Performance Reviews. They Want to Be Compared with Themselves," *Harvard Business Review* (March 22, 2018), https://hbr.org/2018/03/people-dont-want-to-be-compared-with-others-in-performance-reviews-they-want-to-be-compared-with-themselves.

96 greater self-awareness: Sutton et al., "A Longitudinal, Mixed Method Evaluation of Self-Awareness Training in the Workplace."

96 Using your index finger: Silvia and O'Brien, "Self-Awareness and Constructive Functioning."

97 Research has found: Janine Willis and Alexander Todorov, "First Impressions: Making Up Your Mind After a 100-Ms Exposure to a Face," *Psychological Science* 17, no. 7 (July 2006): 592–98, https://doi.org/10.1111/j.1467-9280.2006.01750.x.

97 These judgments don't change: Ibid.

98 The more accurate our assessments: Stephens et al., "High-Quality Connections."

98 when individuals engage: Dierdorff et al., "The Power of Percipience."

98 Menlo Innovations: Stephens et al., "High-Quality Connections."

102 The more someone feels understood: Mortensen and Neeley, "Reflected Knowledge and Trust in Global Collaboration."

102 when you are confident: Ibid.

102 To build organizational awareness: Stephens et al., "High-Quality Connections."

103 Taking time to listen: Ibid.

104 Research finds that behaving: William L. Gardner, Bruce J. Avolio, Fred Luthans, Douglas R. May, and Fred Walumbwa, "'Can You See the Real Me?' A Self-Based Model of Authentic Leader and Follower Development," *Leadership Quarterly* 16, no. 3 (June 2005): 343–72, https://doi.org/10.1016/j.leaqua.2005.03.003.

CHAPTER 5: INFORMAL DEVELOPMENT: HOW WE LEARN TO READ THE AIR

107 the United States military: Wikipedia, "Soft Skills," accessed September 28, 2022, https://en.wikipedia.org/wiki/Soft_skills.

108 Research published in *Harvard Business Review*: Raffaella Sadun, Joseph Fuller, Stephen Hansen, and PJ Neal, "The C-Suite Skills That Matter Most," *Harvard Business Review* (July–August 2022), accessed September 19, 2022, https://hbr.org/2022/07/the-c-suite-skills-that-matter-most.

108 Research has found that 75 percent: Marcel M. Robles, "Executive Perceptions of the Top 10 Soft Skills Needed in Today's Workplace," *Business Communication Quarterly* 75, no. 4 (October 2012): 453–65, https://doi.org/10.1177/1080569912460400.

108 employers rate soft skills: Ibid.

108 *MIT Sloan Management Review* survey: Douglas A. Ready, Carol Cohen, David Kiron, and Benjamin Pring, "The New Leadership Playbook for the Digital Age: Reimagining What It Takes to Lead," *MIT Sloan Management Review* (January 21, 2020), https://sloanreview.mit.edu/projects/the-new-leadership-playbook -for-the-digital-age/.

109 Catalyst in 2010 found: Sabattini and Dinolfo, "Unwritten Rules: Why Doing a Good Job Might Not Be Enough."

114 a 2022 report by McKinsey: Anu Madgavkar, Bill Schaninger, Sven Smit, Jonathan Woetzel, Hamid Samandari, Davis Carlin, Jeongmin Seong, and Kanmani Chockalingam, "Human Capital at Work: The Value of Experience," McKinsey & Company, June 2, 2022, https://www.mckinsey.com/business-functions /people-and-organizational-performance/our-insights/human-capital-at -work-the-value-of-experience.

115 the 2022 McKinsey study: Ibid.

116 a "reskilling emergency": World Economic Forum, "Reskilling Revolution: Preparing 1 Billion People for Tomorrow's Economy," accessed September 19, 2022, https://www.weforum.org/impact/reskilling-revolution/.

116 a 2016 Pew Research study: Jill E. Ellingson and Raymond A. Noe, eds., *Autonomous Learning in the Workplace* (New York: Routledge, 2017).

116 your ability to learn: Allison Littlejohn, Colin Milligan, Rosa Pia Fontana, and Anoush Margaryan, "Professional Learning Through Everyday Work: How Finance Professionals Self-Regulate Their Learning," *Vocations and Learning* 9, no. 2 (January 2016): 207–26, https://doi.org/10.1007/s12186-015-9144-1.

118 Catalyst found in 2010: Sabattini and Dinolfo, "Unwritten Rules: Why Doing a Good Job Might Not Be Enough."

119 first identify examples: Victoria J. Marsick, Karen E. Watkins, Mary Wilson Callahan, and Marie Volpe, "Reviewing Theory and Research on Informal and Incidental Learning," online submission 2006, accessed September 19, 2022, https://eric.ed.gov/?id=ED492754.

120 the primary way: John Cunningham and Emilie Hillier, "Informal Learning in the Workplace: Key Activities and Processes," *Education + Training* 55, no. 1 (February 2013): 37–51, https://doi.org/10.1108/00400911311294960.

120 *most* of our informal learning: Samantha Crans, Veronika Bude, Simon Beausaert, and Mien Segers, "Social Informal Learning and the Role of Learning Climate: Toward a Better Understanding of the Social Side of Learning Among Consultants," *Human Resource Development Quarterly* 32, no. 4 (March 2021): 507–35, https://doi.org/10.1002/hrdq.21429.

126 In the 2016 book *Mindset*: Carol S. Dweck, *Mindset: How We Can Learn to Fulfill Our Potential,* updated edition (London: Hachette UK, January 2017).

126 A 2015 academic research paper: Eva Schürmann and Simon Beausaert, "What Are Drivers for Informal Learning?" *European Journal of Training and Development* 40, no. 3 (April 2016): 130–54, https://doi.org/10.1108/EJTD-06-2015-0044.

127 Your ability to continuously learn: Amelia Manuti, Serafina Pastore, Anna Fausta Scardigno, Maria Luisa Giancaspro, and Daniele Morciano, "Formal and Informal Learning in the Workplace: A Research Review," *International Journal of Training and Development* 19, no. 1 (February 2015): 1–17, https://doi .org/10.1111/ijtd.12044.

CHAPTER 6: INFORMAL ADVANCEMENT: HOW TO MANAGE YOUR CAREER

130 In the 1950s and 1960s: Wong Siew Chin and Roziah Mohd Rasdi, "Protean Career Development: Exploring the Individuals, Organizational and Job-Related

Factors," *Asian Social Science* 10, no. 21 (2014): 203, http:/doi.org/10.5539/ass
.v10n21p203.

130 But fast-forward: Ibid.

130 Careers change so much: Editors of the Encyclopaedia Britannica, "Proteus:
Greek Mythology," *Encyclopedia Britannica*, accessed September 19, 2022,
https://www.britannica.com/topic/Proteus-Greek-mythology.

132 our definition of career success: Liangtie Dai and Fuhui Song, "Subjective Career Success: A Literature Review and Prospect," *Journal of Human Resource
and Sustainability Studies* 4, no. 3 (2016): 238–42, http://doi.org/10.4236
/jhrss.2016.43026.

132 Today, career success: Ibid.

133 employers are more likely: Ibid.

133 When it comes to protean careers: Ilias Kapoutsis, Alexandros Papalexandris,
Ioannis C. Thanos, and Andreas G. Nikolopoulos, "The Role of Political Tactics
on the Organizational Context–Career Success Relationship," *International
Journal of Human Resource Management* 23, no. 9 (2012): 1908–29, https://doi.
org/10.1080/09585192.2011.610345.

133 Career success today: Dai and Song, "Subjective Career Success: A Literature
Review and Prospect."

133 In protean careers: Douglas T. Hall, Jeffrey Yip, and Kathryn Doiron, "Protean
Careers at Work: Self-Direction and Values Orientation in Psychological Success," *Annual Review of Organizational Psychology and Organizational Behavior*
5 (2018): 129–56, https://doi.org/10.1146/annurev-orgpsych-032117-104631.

134 A 2009 academic study: Tracy Levett-Jones and Judith Lathlean, "The As-
cent to Competence Conceptual Framework: An Outcome of a Study of Belongingness," *Journal of Clinical Nursing* 18, no. 20 (2009): 2870–79, http://doi
.org/10.1111/j.1365-2702.2008.02593.x.

135 Quiet quitting: Jack Zenger and Joseph Folkman, "Quiet Quitting Is About Bad
Bosses, Not Bad Employees," *Harvard Business Review* (August 31, 2022), https://
hbr.org/2022/08/quiet-quitting-is-about-bad-bosses-not-bad-employees.

136 a 2022 study: Anita Gaile, Ilona Baumane-Vītoliņa, Kurmet Kivipõld, and
Agnis Stibe, "Examining Subjective Career Success of Knowledge Workers,"
Review of Managerial Science (2022): 1–26, https://doi.org/10.1007/s11846
-022-00523-x.

136 managers who supported employees: Ibid.

137 The more your needs are met: Ibid.

137 It is difficult to measure: Gallup, "State of the Global Workplace: 2022 Report,"
accessed September 19, 2022, https://www.gallup.com/workplace/349484
/state-of-the-global-workplace-2022-report.aspx#ite-393245.

137 Participants in this study: Ibid.

138 A 2021 study: Gaile et al., "Examining Subjective Career Success of Knowledge
Workers."

138 A 2022 academic study: Hui Li, Hang-yue Ngo, and Francis Cheung, "Linking
Protean Career Orientation and Career Decidedness: The Mediating Role of
Career Decision Self-Efficacy," *Journal of Vocational Behavior* 115 (December
2019): 103322, https://doi.org/10.1016/j.jvb.2019.103322.

139 individuals who are clear about: Ibid.

139 careers don't unfold: Gaile et al., "Examining Subjective Career Success of
Knowledge Workers."

140 career satisfaction is typically lower: Margaret Yap, Wendy Cukier, Mark
Holmes, and Charity-Ann Hannan, "Career Satisfaction: A Look Behind the
Races," *Relations Industrielles/Industrial Relations* 65, no. 4 (2010): 584–608,
https://www.jstor.org/stable/23078321.

140 employee career satisfaction: Ibid.

140 a manager's inclusive leadership behaviors: J. Travis, Emily Shaffer, and Jennifer Thorpe-Moscon, "Getting Real About Inclusive Leadership (Report)," Catalyst, November 21, 2019, https://www.catalyst.org/research/inclusive-leadership-report/.

140 the more you take action: Andreas Hirschi and Jessie Koen, "Contemporary Career Orientations and Career Self-Management: A Review and Integration," *Journal of Vocational Behavior* 126 (April 2021): 103505, https://doi.org/10.1016/j.jvb.2020.103505.

141 Instead, career management: Mel Fugate, Angelo J. Kinicki, and Blake E. Ashforth, "Employability: A Psycho-Social Construct, Its Dimensions, and Applications," *Journal of Vocational Behavior* 65, no. 1 (2004): 14–38, https://doi.org/10.1016/j.jvb.2003.10.005.

141 the more employable you are: Ibid.

142 most articles agree: Gaile et al., "Examining Subjective Career Success of Knowledge Workers."

142 career satisfaction isn't a result: Ibid.

143 *ikigai* encompasses all elements of life: Toshimasa Sone, Naoki Nakaya, Kaori Ohmori, Taichi Shimazu, Mizuka Higashiguchi, Masako Kakizaki, Nobutaka Kikuchi, Shinichi Kuriyama, and Ichiro Tsuji, "Sense of Life Worth Living (Ikigai) and Mortality in Japan: Ohsaki Study," *Psychosomatic Medicine* 70, no. 6 (July 2008): 709–15, http://doi.org/10.1097/PSY.0b013e31817e7e64.

143 A 2008 research study: Ibid.

145 Why statements are powerful: Gaile et al., "Examining Subjective Career Success of Knowledge Workers."

145 boundaryless protean career: Lillian T. Eby, Marcus Butts, and Angie Lockwood, "Predictors of Success in the Era of the Boundaryless Career," *Journal of Organizational Behavior* 24, no. 6 (August 2003): 689–708, https://doi.org/10.1002/job.214.

146 The term *mentor*: Tammy D. Allen, Lillian T. Eby, Mark L. Poteet, Elizabeth Lentz, and Lizzette Lima, "Career Benefits Associated with Mentoring for Protégés: A Meta-Analysis," *Journal of Applied Psychology* 89, no. 1 (2004): 127, https://doi.org/10.1037/0021-9010.89.1.127.

147 why men advance at work: Benjamin Artz, Amanda Goodall, and Andrew J. Oswald, "Research: Women Ask for Raises as Often as Men, but Are Less Likely to Get Them," *Harvard Business Review* (June 25, 2018), https://hbr.org/2018/06/research-women-ask-for-raises-as-often-as-men-but-are-less-likely-to-get-them.

147 Despite companies investing: Marissa King, *Social Chemistry: Decoding the Patterns of Human Connection* (New York: Dutton, 2022).

148 The problem with informal mentoring: Belle Rose Ragins, "Diversity and Workplace Mentoring Relationships: A Review and Positive Social Capital Approach," in *The Blackwell Handbook of Mentoring: A Multiple Perspectives Approach*, eds. Tammy D. Allen and Lillian T. Eby (West Sussex, UK: Wiley-Blackwell, 2007), 281–300.

148 Mentoring and sponsorship work: Rick Woolworth, "Great Mentors Focus on the Whole Person, Not Just Their Career," *Harvard Business Review* (August 9, 2019), https://hbr.org/2019/08/great-mentors-focus-on-the-whole-person-not-just-their-career.

149 Numerous studies: Sylvia Ann Hewlett Associates, "White Paper: Advocacy vs. Mentoring," accessed September 19, 2022, https://www.cisco.com/c/dam/en_us/about/ac49/ac55/docs/Advocacy_vs_Mentoring_white_paper.pdf.

149 A 2016 academic research study: Kelly Campbell, Nicole Holderness, and Matt Riggs, "Friendship Chemistry: An Examination of Underlying Factors," *So-

cial Science Journal 52, no. 2 (February 2015): 239–47, http://doi.org/10.1016/j
.soscij.2015.01.005.

150 when you support another person's advancement: Heather Foust-Cummings,
Sarah Dinolfo, and Jennifer Kohler, "Sponsoring Women to Success (Report),"
Catalyst, August 17, 2011, https://www.catalyst.org/research/sponsoring
-women-to-success/.

151 Know-how is about understanding: Robert Zinko and Mark Rubin, "Personal
Reputation and the Organization," *Journal of Management & Organization* 21,
no. 2 (January 2015): 217–36, http://doi.org/10.1017/jmo.2014.76.

151 knowing how to manage your reputation: Ibid.

151 A CEO's reputation: Ibid.

152 The 2017 academic study: Robert Zinko, Zhan Zhang Furner, James Hunt, and
Adam Dalton, "Establishing a Reputation," *Journal of Employment Counseling*
54, no. 2 (June 2017): 87–96.

155 protean careers make us better coworkers: Hall et al., "Protean Careers at Work:
Self-Direction and Values Orientation in Psychological Success."

156 When your needs are met: Ibid.

CHAPTER 7: PAY IT FORWARD: HOW TO FIND MEANING AT WORK

157 when leaders talk: John Nemo, "What a NASA Janitor Can Teach Us About Living
a Bigger Life," Business Journals, December 23, 2014, https://www.bizjournals
.com/bizjournals/how-to/growth-strategies/2014/12/what-a-nasa-janitor
-can-teach-us.html.

158 A 2020 study: Decha Dechawatanapaisal, "Meaningful Work on Career Satisfaction: A Moderated Mediation Model of Job Embeddedness and Work-Based
Social Support," *Management Research Review* 44, no. 6 (2020): 889–908,
https://doi.org/10.1108/MRR-06-2020-0308.

158 how we find meaning: Ibid.

159 For work to be truly meaningful: Michael F. Steger, "Creating Meaning and Purpose at Work," in *The Wiley Blackwell Handbook of the Psychology of Positivity
and Strengths-Based Approaches at Work*, eds. Lindsay G. Oades, Michael Steger,
Antonella Delle Fave, and John Passmore (West Sussex, UK: John Wiley & Sons,
2016), 60–81.

159 Despite the common myth: Stewart I. Donaldson and Scott I. Donaldson, "Other
People Matter: The Power of Positive Relationships," in *Toward a Positive Psy-
chology of Relationships: New Directions in Theory and Research*, eds. Meg A.
Warren and Stewart I. Donaldson (Santa Barbara, CA: Praeger, 2018), 1–8.

159 A 2014 review: Stewart I. Donaldson, Maren Dollwet, and Meghana A. Rao,
"Happiness, Excellence, and Optimal Human Functioning Revisited: Examining the Peer-Reviewed Literature Linked to Positive Psychology," *Journal of
Positive Psychology* 10, no. 3 (August 2014): 85–195, https://doi.org/10.1080/174
39760.2014.943801.

159 2018 study by BetterUp: Shawn Achor, Andrew Reece, Gabriella Rosen Kellerman, and Alexi Robichaux, "9 Out of 10 People Are Willing to Earn Less Money
to Do More-Meaningful Work," *Harvard Business Review* (November 6, 2018),
https://hbr.org/2018/11/9-out-of-10-people-are-willing-to-earn-less-money
-to-do-more-meaningful-work.

160 employees pay it forward: Daniel S. Whitman, David L. Van Rooy, and Chockalingam Viswesvaran, "Satisfaction, Citizenship Behaviors, and Performance
in Work Units: A Meta-Analysis of Collective Construct Relations," *Personnel
Psychology* 63, no. 1 (February 2010): 41–81, https://doi.org/10.1111/j.1744
-6570.2009.01162.x.

160 people voluntarily help others: Theresa Eriksson and Caitlin Ferreira, "Who Pays It Forward the Most? Examining Organizational Citizenship Behavior in the Workplace," *Journal of Theoretical Social Psychology* 5, no. 3 (February 2021): 215–28, https://doi.org/10.1002/jts5.87.

161 A 2020 academic study: Ibid.

162 there are generally two ways: Wayne E. Baker and Nathaniel Bulkley, "Paying It Forward versus Rewarding Reputation: Mechanisms of Generalized Reciprocity," *Organization Science* 25, no. 5 (April 2014): 1493–510, https://doi.org/10.1287/orsc.2014.0920.

163 the more help a person receives: Ibid.

163 A 2014 research study: Eriksson and Ferreira, "Who Pays It Forward the Most?"

165 Winds of Fate: Ella Wheeler Wilcox, "The Winds of Fate," Public Domain Poetry, accessed September 19, 2022, https://www.public-domain-poetry.com/ella-wheeler-wilcox/winds-of-fate-32784.

165 we are less concerned: Philip H. Mirvis and Douglas T. Hall, "Psychological Success and the Boundaryless Career," *Journal of Organizational Behavior* 15, no. 4 (July 1994): 365–80, https://doi.org/10.1002/job.4030150406.

165 organizational development scholar: Herb Shepard, "A Path with a Heart: The Cultural Context of Learning About Careers," Scribd, accessed September 28, 2022, https://www.scribd.com/document/134126758/Shepard-1984-Chosing-a-Path-With-Heart.

166 Your career success and fulfillment: Gaile et al., "Examining Subjective Career Success of Knowledge Workers."

INDEX

ABOUT THE AUTHOR

Dr. Michelle Penelope King is a globally recognized expert on inequality and organizational culture. Based on over a decade's worth of research, Michelle believes that learning to read the air is the most important thing we can do to future-proof our careers. She is the host of a popular podcast called *The Fix*. Michelle is the author of the bestselling, award-winning book *The Fix: Overcome the Invisible Barriers That Are Holding Women Back at Work*.

Michelle has been featured in the *Economist*, *Harvard Business Review*, CNBC, CNN Business, *Fortune*, *Financial Times*, Bloomberg, *Time*, *Business Insider*, the *Times*, the *Daily Mail*, and LinkedIn Editors.

Michelle is the founder of The Culture Practice, a global consultancy that provides leaders with the assessment, development, and inclusion coaching needed to build cultures that value difference. In addition, Michelle is a senior advisor to the UN Foundation's Girl Up Campaign, where she leads the NextGen Leadership Development Program, which enables young women to navigate and overcome the barriers to their success. Before this, Michelle was the director of inclusion at Netflix. Prior to that, she was the head of the UN Women's Global Innovation Coalition for Change, which includes managing over thirty private-sector partnerships to accelerate the achievement of gender equality and women's empowerment. Michelle has two decades of international experience working in the private sector.

In each of her roles, Michelle lends her expertise to advance gender equality and enhance global opportunity and achievement for women.

In 2022, Michelle was named LinkedIn's Top Voice for Equity in the Workplace and was recognized as one of the 100 Women @ Davos by Global Women's Leadership Experts. In addition, in 2019, Women Tech Founders, a Chicago-based organization dedicated to advancing women in the tech industry, awarded Michelle its Inspiring Innovator Award for her outstanding achievements in the sector.

Michelle is a published, award-winning academic with a bachelor of arts in industrial organizational psychology, a master of arts in industrial-organizational psychology, a master of business administration, a postgraduate degree in journalism, and a PhD in management. Michelle is pursuing a postdoctoral research fellowship at Cranfield University in the United Kingdom.